FRANCIS BOLA AKIN-JOHN

GUEST MINISTERS TODAY

HOW THEY CAN HELP OR HINDER
YOUR CHURCH / MINISTRY

Guest Ministers Today

ISBN 978-9783854062

All Scripture quotations are from King James Version of the Bible, unless otherwise stated.

Published by:

CHURCH
GROWTH
SERVICES INC.

332, Abeokuta Expresswy, By Super Bus Stop, Oke-Odo, Agege, Lagos
Tel.: 234-01-8976100, 08023000714, 08029744296
E-mail: akingrow@yahoo.com
www: churchgrowthafrica.org

Printed in Nigeria by:
LIFE & MINISTRY PUBLICATIONS
Tel.: 234-1-7934133, (0)8037152451

CONTENTS

DEDICATION

To those faithful and loyal ministers who have
genuinely built the body of Christ over the years
with their itinerant ministries. God bless you
now and always.

APPRECIATION

Who else can I give eternal thanks, praise and adoration to, than the Almighty God? Thank you Lord for your Spirit that enabled me to write this book in just five days while I was away in Paris. Thank you Lord for the Scriptural insights and revelations.

My appreciation goes to Prof. Watto, a dynamic Pastor of Pastors in Paris who housed and fed me for one week and provided a quiet and conducive place for me to write this book. Merci Papa!

I thank my associate, Rev Michael Oluwaniyi for faithfully holding forth at home. The ministry staff: Pastor Joseph Daniels, Pastor Femi Awolesi, Kemi Aina, Tosin Badmus and others. Thanks a lot.

I thank Evang. Adedeji Adekusibe for the silent work for the Lord and Rev. Dr. Tunde Tanimomo for the good job of proof-reading and correction. I also thank my printer, Rev Biola Longe and all those who contributed in one way or the other to make this book possible. God bless you all real goooood!

My unreserved thanks goes to my wife, Kemi and the boys for enduring my absence. God bless you now and always.

Every grace to you today.

PREFACE

Having closely worked, walked and related with Dr. Francis Bola Akin-John for well over a decade now, I can as a friend, scholar, mentoree and particularly an admirer of goodness of God in the lives of people, say he has a special endowment of the Grace of God.

The art of speaking is far different from the art of writing. To have a command of both arts of speaking and writing therefore is no doubt a rare grace of God he enjoys. His art of writing could however be traced to the wealth of experiences he has gathered in his wide reading, extensive travelling, solid connection and free and open relationship with people.

You hardly find published works of critics in the market because of their fear of being criticised. But I have found Dr. Bola Akin-John as a fearless and purposeful author whose works have served as mirror to challenge the deeply decaying sores and foxes that stand in whatever capacity to ruin the vineyards and body of Christ.

Pick any of his books at anytime, from anywhere you can find it, and it will serve as panacea to any problem you may have; especially this Guest Minister.

Evang. Dr. Tunde Tanimomo
President & Rector,
Christ International School of Evangelism.
An Arm of 'The Vine Restoration Evangelistic Ministries
Int.' Adalemo, Sango-Ota, Ogun State, Nigeria.

INTRODUCTION

I have come to discover that there is silent crisis going on in most churches and ministries today. It is the crisis of guest speakers. It is both negative and positive in nature, but the scale tilt more towards the negative side. church and ministry leaders are largely mute about this crisis, but nobody can deny its existence. Quite unfortunately, it has consumed many ministries and presently, many church leaders are trying to grapple with this problem. Well, I hope this book can be of real help to such leaders. Permit me to itemise some of the reasons for this book.

1. Ministry and church leader have kept quiet for too long:

There is scanty teaching, book, emphasis and warning about guest ministers in most of our schools of ministry, Bible schools and ministers conferences. This has allowed many church leaders to do whatever they like and guest ministers have had a field day milking and short-changing churches.

It is not a problem that started yesterday, it has been going on for years, but most top leaders have failed to really speak out as they should. Though, there have been some warnings in few denominational churches about the type of guest minister they should allow, but largely across the board, topmost church leaders have been too quiet on this issue. This is the gap that this book have come to adequately fill.

2.   Many ungodly practises abound by guest ministers:

Since there are little or no guidelines and ethics to follow, most invited speakers usually takes the law into their hands and do things that mostly benefit themselves and not the church of Jesus Christ. I know churches that got scattered and in disarray due to the ungodly antics of invited speakers.

A guest minister was invited to a church to preach. He did a good job and warm his way into the heart of the people. Before you could bat an eyelid, he started messing around with the women. He was sent away shamefully, but the church never remained the same too. Many aggrieved people left and the church had to start from the scratch all over again. This is a tip of the numerous atrocities being perpetrated by invited speakers in churches and ministries today. The aim of this book is to reduce these problems to the bearest minimum.

3.   Many ministers now run invitation ministry only:

I'm aware and have seen many ministers who have no ministry base anywhere and they only thrive on welcoming invitations to preach in churches and ministry functions only. They are freelance and mobile ministers. Many of them are in the prophetic, evangelistic, apostolic and music ministries. They move from meetings to meetings, preaching and ministering here and there, without any good and stable work of their own. Many of such mobile ministers have little work going on within, yet they boast of great things outside and make merchandise of God's people.

Of course, there is a place for itinerant ministry, but not to the neglect of doing something worthwhile back home before you move out to honour invitations. Many of such ministers who operate invitation ministry only are money mongers. Their desire and motive is money, not really being a blessing to the people of God. It is such 'ministers' that charge for meetings and raise offerings and special seeds for the 'man of God'. If the honorarium is not what they expect, they get angry and demand for more, because they knew how much they've raised. Well, it has become a business venture, not really the work of God again. This book hopes to bring the needed balance to this crucial area.

4. Bad image for Nigerian ministers abroad:

In my several travels across Africa, Europe and Asia, you must have to prove that you are genuine and honest, because of the notoriety of Nigerian ministers who have gone to these places as guest ministers and sometimes, church founders.

In Shoshanguve, Pretoria, in South Africa. I was shown many churches that were scattered due to the immoral and ungodly monetary practises of visiting Nigerian ministers. In Nairobi, Zambia, Ghana, Swaziland, Tanzania and

Europe, it is the same story all over. There are Nigerian ministers who have nothing on ground back at home, but they travelled out to minister, rake money and sleep with women.

In some cases, they broke away their host churches to start their own and re-marry so as to perfect their stay over there, even though they have wives and kids back home in Nigeria. The situation is so bad that we have to start serving as a clearance base for some churches. I pray that God will use this book to arrest this ungodly trend and repair the bad image that the average Nigerian preacher have come to attract.

5.   Churches are being run by guest speakers:

I've known and seen so many churches being run and constantly lead by one guest speaker or the other. It's as if the host Pastors have abdicated their God given responsibility to visiting ministers. There are even churches founded by 'rich guys' that are not called by God. So, they run the church by inviting one guest speaker or the other for various meetings, week in, week out. Some pastors are always on the look out for guest speakers, and they invite anybody to their church, so long he or she can preach, even if the Invited Speaker doesn't have a semblance of godliness.

These and many other reasons that you 'll be reading necessitate the writing of this book. This is an issue that is so practical and widespread among many churches, that someone need to speak up about all the abuses being practised today.

Of course, I'm also a guest speaker in many churches and ministry related events, and I've had to put up with lots of strange practises by my hosts, while trying to put these things into consideration. Yet, we must practise the truths in this book. Either you are a guest minister somewhere or you are the host minister, this book have something for everyone, and if you are open-minded enough, you can pick one or two things that will greatly help your ministry and ministrations.

Every grace to you today.

Dr. Francis Bola Akin-John
May 2007.

CHAPTER 1

BASIS AND QUALITIES
OF GUEST MINISTERS

A church was started by some brethren that were driven out of a particular church. They invited a pastor to lead them. The man of God struggled with the church for some few years due to infighting, bickering and disunity among the brethren. At last, prayers for revival was started by some brothers, and after a period of time, a guest minister was invited by the church through clear leading of the Lord.

When he came, the Lord started working mightily through him. Many were revived, restoration was made, sinners came to know the Lord, backsliders were restored and the church grew both in quantity and quality. Many Christians were filled with the Holy Spirit and the church was alive and well again. The meetings continued for weeks and many miracles were experienced. The church was never the same again. Today, many of the Christians of that meeting have become pastors and ministers of the gospel. This true life story is the model of what guest ministers should be in churches and ministries.

As a form of definition, a guest minister is a true and genuine servant of God; someone who has something to give to others; someone who has been touched by the Lord and can be a channel of God's power and blessing to others. A guest minister must be someone who has walked with the Lord and is ready to share, educate, impact and empower others with the fire and insight he has received from the Lord. A guest minister is someone who had developed an expertise in an area and has results to show to others that it works. A guest minister is someone who has the definite hand of God upon his life and he can therefore lead people into the very presence of God by his words, prayers and life.

Not every minister, pastor, teacher or bishop qualifies to be a good and effective guest speaker, according to these definitions. Many can only offer head knowledge and theory of God, but cannot lead people into true and genuine relationship with the Lord. A good guest minister is not necessarily an orator, but

> *A guest minister is someone who had developed an expertise in an area and has results to show to others that it works*

someone with the life, integrity, power and presence of God in his or her life.

SCRIPTURAL FOUNDATION

Biblically speaking, there is a place for inviting fellow ministers to share and lead the people with the host pastor. Exchange of pulpits or bringing in guest ministers should be a normal and natural practise in the church among ministers, no matter our denominational affiliation. Apostle Peter was a good guest minister.

> *"Now when the Apostles which were at Jerusalem heard that Samaria had received the word of God, they sent unto them Peter and John: who, when they were come down, prayed for them, that they might receive the Holy Ghost".* (Acts 8:14-15).

> *"And now send men to Joppa, and call for one Simon, whose surname is Peter: he lodgeth with one Simon a tanner, whose house is by the sea side: he shall tell thee what thou oughtest to do " ... while Peter yet spake these words, the Holy Ghost fell on all them which heard the word. And they of the circumcision which believed were astonished, as many came with Peter, because that on the Gentiles, also*

were poured out the gift of the Holy Ghost" (Acts 10:5-6,44-45).

Peter was always a heaven sent guest minister wherever he goes or was sent. He always brought divine dimension to the work of his host. In fact, heaven recommended him to churches and leaders as someone who can lead them to the next level of God's plan. May we be such guest ministers in Jesus' name. Peter and John helped the work of Philip to get better. Every church needs such guest ministers once in a while to bring the fresh dimension of God and refreshing presence of the Lord to the people. There will always be a place for that in the Ministry.

> *Peter was always a heaven sent guest minister wherever he goes or was sent. He always brought divine dimension to the work of his host*

Denominations that don't welcome guest ministers from outside are short-changing themselves. I'm aware that many churches take the decision of not inviting or welcoming guest ministers from outside because of past nasty experiences, yet, the truth is that the church will be missing the special blessings of God that outside speakers can bring.

QUALITIES OF A GUEST MINISTER

Every Guest Minister must be true men and women of God.

"And a certain Jew named Apollos, born at Alexandra, an eloquent man, and mighty in the Scriptures, came to Ephesus. This man was instructed in the way of the Lord: and being fervent in the spirit, he spake and taught diligently the things of the Lord, knowing only the baptism of John. And he began to speak bodly in the synagogue: whom when Aquila and Priscilla had the way of God more perfectly. And when he was disposed to pass unto Achaia, the brethren wrote, exhorting the disciples to receive him: who when he was come helped them much which had believed through grace" (Acts 18:24-27).

From this account of Apollos, we can deduce several qualities that guest ministers must possess:

i.   **He must be someone who knows the Lord intimately.** A speaker that doesn't know the Lord will do more damage than good to the church.

ii. **He must be someone who is spiritual and fervent in the Lord.** An unspiritual man in a spiritual work will spell disaster of great proportion.

iii. **He must be someone who had been properly taught.** He that has not been taught is not fit to teach others.

iv. **He must be someone who is deep in the word of God, not ideas of man.** Edifying the church with the word of God is the goal of inviting Guest Speakers. God will only bless His word, not the ideas of men.

v. **He must be someone who is willing to learn.** Whoever that has not learned and continue to learn is not fit to teach others.

vi. **He must be someone who is gifted and anointed.** Gift and anointing will magnetise people always.

vii. **He must be someone who has a heart to help.** Wrong motives disqualifies a man from helping others sincerely.

viii. **He must be someone who is ready to be corrected.** Stubborn and proud speakers will d o more harm than good to the life of the people of God.

ix. **He must not be a controversial or troublesome person.** A controversial person will bring more crisis than progress to the work.

x. **He must be someone who is dependable and trust-worthy.** A speaker that is not credible will destroy your work if you give him your pulpit.

xi. **He must be someone who is simple, open**

and uncomplicated. Greedy and difficult to please people should never be allowed to speak in your church.

xii.   **He must be someone who is willing to submit to the host pastor.** Whoever is too proud to submit and humble himself or herself under the host Pastor is not fit to lead your people.

xiii. **He must be someone whose character can be attested to by credible leaders**. A person with bad testimonies and evil reports here and there will bring untold damage to your work.

xiv.   **He must be someone who has a base for ministry recommendation.** Anyone who doesn't have a base and cannot be vouched for should not mount your pulpit.

By prayer, patience, witness of the Spirit and careful investigation, you can always know the speakers who possess these qualities and worthy of being invited to your church or ministry

Whoever wants to be a guest minister in biblical way must live and imbibe these qualities into his or her life. Whenever you want to invite guest ministers, these are the things you must look for in his life. If he doesn't possess these qualities, you dare not invite him. If you do, you might be destroying the work you've laboured to build for years. You may ask; how can I know those who have these qualities? By prayer, patience, witness of the Spirit and careful investigation, you can always know the speakers who possess these qualities and worthy of being invited to your church or ministry.

Apollos is a good example of a guest speaker. He possessed all the above-mentioned qualities. Every guest speaker must measure up to this biblical standard.

CHAPTER 2

PURPOSE AND PLACE

OF GUEST MINISTERS

A particular church had grown over the years. Good membership and favour of God was upon the church. Members have been blessed by God and many of them had been lifted from penury to material and financial prosperity. But there is a problem. The love of the people for evangelism, outreach, mission and soul winning had waned and lukewarmness had set in.

After much prayer, the Pastor was led to invite a dynamic evangelist to the church for a week indoor meeting, with the sole intention of reviving the evangelism and mission zeal of the people. The evangelist did a good job and God was mightily with him. Before the week ran out, the fire of evangelism, mission and soul winning had been re-kindled in the heart of the people. Many re-dedicated their lives, time, talent and treasures to reaching out to the lost. Many souls were also saved and the church was alive again with the fire and zeal of soul winning.

Without doubt, this is the true example of the purpose of guest ministers in a church or Ministry related events. guest ministers must not be invited whimsically, rather, they must be purposely invited to fulfil a certain objective in the church or ministry. Beware, guest ministers have the capacity to make or mar your work.

THE PLACE OF GUEST MINISTERS

Many hands make large work. Nobody can run a ministry or lead a church alone. You will always need the input and contribution of other leaders and ministers. Every genuine and sincere servant of the Lord must welcome carefully chosen ministers to help him in the work. Every Stephen will need the gift and ministry of Peter and John in their work. Every Cornelius will need the input of a Peter if God must lead and lift the church to her next level of blessings. The ministry of a certain Apollos will always be needed by other churches and leaders.

The reality however is that no minister or leader, no matter how anointed and close to God he is, can build a great work alone

I've met and observed leaders who don't believe in this truth. They labour alone and build the ministry on themselves. They pray, teach, train and develop the people and the work alone. They work with the notion that God has given them all that will make the work to move to the next level. Well, the truth is that such leaders will eventually build imbalanced work and ministry. In very many cases, the work get stuck at a point and every effort to move it forward will fail.

The reality however is that no minister or leader, no matter how anointed and close to God he is, can build a great work alone. You will always need the input, advise, counsel, insight and fresh dimension that God can bring to you through the ministry of another minister. This was the case with Moses in the wilderness.

> *"And Jethro, Moses' father-in-law took a burnt offering and sacrifices for God: and Aaron came, and all the elders of Israel, to eat bread with Moses' father-in-law before God. And it came to pass on the morrow that Moses sat to judge the people; and the people stood by Moses from the morning unto the evening. And when Moses' father-in-law saw all that he did to the people, he said, what is this that thou doest to the people? Why sittest thou thyself alone, and all the people stand by thee from morning unto even? ... And Moses' father in law*

said unto him, the thing that thou doest is not good. Thou wilt surely wear away, both thou, and this people that is with thee: for this thing is too heavy for thee; thou art not able to perform it thyself alone" (Exodus 18:12-14, 17-18).

Moses thought he could do it alone without the contribution of another person. But his father-in-law brought him the dimension that will lead his ministry to the next level. Father Jethro brought outsider's perspective to the work of Moses. Thank God, Moses did not reject this golden and timely insight, else, his ministry would have been stuck at that point. The lesson? Every leader needs an outsider's perspective in his work. To say it in our context, you need the input of a dynamic and experienced guest minister, if your work will really move to the next level. Churches and ministries that close their doors against worthwhile guest ministers are simply closing their doors against their next level in ministry.

THE PURPOSE OF GUEST MINISTERS

However, be that as it may, not every Dick and Harry, Tom and Jerry that call themselves ministers or speakers should be invited to your church or ministry. Neither should you attend the conferences, seminars and trainings of every advertised speaker. You must carefully choose and prayerfully examine every minister on merit. What are the general purposes of every guest minister in a church or ministry function?

> The purpose of guest ministers is to bring revival, renewal and revitalisation to the faith of the people

a.   To re-emphasise what the host minister has been emphasising

Sometimes, the people need an outside speaker to confirm what the host minister had been teaching. Guest ministers are not to teach doctrines, but to simply ground the people in the truth that they have been hearing from their leaders. It is simply to let the people hear the old truth from another source and dimension.

b.   To bring some freshness and vitality to the work

The purpose of guest ministers is to bring revival, renewal and revitalisation to the faith of the people. Restoration to backsliders, salvation to hypocrites, healing to the sick and fresh fire and zeal to those who are lukewarm are the hallmark of guest ministration in churches. Fresh obedience to God's word and renewed relationship with God must be the outcome of the ministration of a Guest minister in the church.

c.   To help the work and church to greater level

The purpose of bringing in a guest minister is so that the work can be helped to greater level as a result of his ministration and prayers. This is the scriptural testimony of father Jethro to Moses, Peter to Philip and Apollos to the churches. Guest ministers that leave the church scattered, poorer and disunited than they met it are devilish. Every guest minister must pray, fast, study, prepare and minister in such a way to leave the people more blessed, edified and better than they met them. It is then and only then they are fufilling their biblical purposes.

A guest minister was once invited to a church. He really brought the power and presence of God never before seen in that church. He preached the truth, prayed for the sick and minister in such a power ful way that the spiritual temperature of the church ran to an all time high. Amazing healings took place and many people were soundly saved to the extent that the attendance of few hundreds jumped to thousands, even after he left. That is the divine purpose for every guest minister.

d. To bring some expertise in the ways and things of God

Guest ministers that are experts in some areas must help the church to become better. Guest ministers that have acquired expertise through trainings, calling, experience and walking with God can help the church in the area of church growth, health, discipleship, leadership, equipping the under- leaders and generally helping the work to avoid stagnation, crisis, downward-spiral and retrogression. More than ever before, every church and ministry needs guest ministers who can fulfil this purpose in the kingdom of God.

With due sense of humility and praise to God, I've been able to function in this area to many pastors, churches and denominations across the world in the last few years. And I still have many years to offer the body of Christ by God's special grace. Guest ministers should bring growth and progress to the church, not crisis and retardation.

e. To assist the host minister in building a better and greater work

Guest ministers must work with and alongside their host ministers, not over and above them. I've seen several cases of guest ministers undermining the authority, influence and integrity of their host ministers. This is absolutely wrong and ungodly. Guest ministers must be under the authority of their host pastor, while they are ministering in his church and their purpose must be to help the host pastor build a greater work for the Lord. Any guest minister that can't fulfil this purpose should honourably quit and return back to his base. Pronto! Rather than undermine your host, quit and go back home. Mountain climbers must help each other, not undermining one another.

> *Guest ministers must work with and alongside their host ministers, not over and above them*

Guest Ministers can be great blessings and not a curse to the church if we abide by these purposes. Either you are inviting a guest minister or you are a guest minister yourself, you must constantly keep these purpose at heart and let them guide your conduct and ministrations.

The kingdom of God will become better if we all live and abide by these five purposes. These are the purposes and job description of every guest minister, where ever they are.

C H A P T E R 3

THE PLACE OF

THE HOST MINISTER

A pastor once narrated his experience to me. He was always in the habit of inviting a particular guest minister to his church. He comes every now and then to hold and conduct one service or the other. At a point, the guest minister was so regular that you'll be forgiven if you mistake him for the host pastor. He was trusted to the extent that the host pastor will leave the church in his care, while he attended to his business concerns.

The guest minister so entrenched himself in the church and when he eventually decided to start his own church nearby few months later, ninety five percent of the members followed him. The host minister had to start all over again after learning his lesson the hard way. Moreover, I have to say that this is not an isolated case, but a re-occuring problem in the church today. It has become a frustrating reality in many churches today.

> *Every pastor must be dynamic, relevant and current in the church*

The host minister must be the leader in the church. Call him any name; President, Pastor, Founder, General Overseer, Bishop or Apostle, he must be the man of God responsible for the church. God doesn't work in a vacuum. He works through one man; chosen and commissioned by Him. That man is responsible for the church. As a leader or shepherd, he must lead, feed, guide and nurture the sheep in the ways of the Lord. He must be capable, competent and effective. Paul told Timothy, who was then the pastor of the church in Corinth:

> *"Study to shew thy self approved unto God, a workman that needeth not to be ashamed, rightly dividing the word of truth"* (II Tim. 2:5).

Every pastor must be dynamic, relevant and current in the church. The pastor must be God's man, in God's place and at God's time. He must be knowledgeable and competent enough that his people will have implicit confidence in him.

Balanced and durable ministry demands that the host pastor must be resourceful enough to feed and nurture the people systematically in the word of God. Sheep only graze where the grass is green. The host pastor must continually provide a green grass for the people, if they are to continue to graze under his shepherdship.

Therefore, the pastor must learn, improve, change and equip himself until he is a reservoir of timely and relevant truth of God's word to the extent that his people will be happy to hear him always with or without guest speakers. This had been my experience in ministry, both while I was pastoring and in church growth work. People initially told me to invite big name speakers to our conferences, but I refused and decided to build up myself. Today, it has paid off. Host pastors that refuse to build up themselves will be at the mercy of guest ministers, and their work will be the worse for it.

ABSENTEE PASTORS

Because of economic reasons, many pastors of small churches are bi-vocational today. That means they have to keep a job and spend their spare time pastoring their struggling churches. We should praise and encourage such pastors. However, solid and quality work will only be done in the life of the people when the pastor is really available to lead, pastor, nurture and equip the people in the things of the Lord.

Host pastors that refuse to build up themselves will be at the mercy of guest ministers, and their work will be the worse for it

I always recommend that one should be a bi-vocational pastor when the work is small and under eighty adult members. But after that, the pastor must become full time, so that he can spend time in prayers, studying, visiting and nurturing the people for God. Nurturing people and building a solid work requires time. Investment of time and effort is the price for quality work.

Amazingly, too many pastors of this jet age don't want to do this. Even though they are around, the truth is that they are not available to nurture the people. Many pastors are absentee pastors. They move here and there, doing one meeting or the other for other churches and ministries and they left their own church uncared for.

I know quite a number of such pitiable pastors. They accept invitations to minister all through the week and months. They hardly stay at home. Why? Because the invitations will fetch them more personal money than their churches! What a mercantile spirit! In 52 Sundays in a year, they hardly stay in their churches more than 20 Sundays. Small wonder those churches are famished and once they see a good guest speaker, they move away with him *enmasse*!

Pastors must be in their churches to nurture, empower and equip the people to be true disciples of the Lord. Pastors who are too busy to be available or to attend to the spiritual and psychological needs of their members will always experience breakaway. Guest ministers can always make a mince-meat of your people, once you are not available to nurture them for the Lord. People that are unstable, babyish and immature in the Lord can always be tossed to and fro by guest speakers with ulterior motives. People who are not properly nurtured and grounded in the Lord will be carried about with every wind of doctrine and bad Guest Speakers can use them to fester their own nets.

Constant transfer of pastors or change of pulpits in denominational churches doesn't really help the growth of local churches

While writing this book in a seminary professor's house in France, a pastor visited and I asked why his church where I preached the previous Sunday was small. He related the story of how a visiting guest speaker instigated his associate minister against him and took away many members to start his own church in the town, but the church closed down six months later. The people scattered and many of them cannot come back to the church because of the shame of what they had done. Proper nurturing and teaching would have prevented that or reduced it to the bearest minimum.

Furthermore, constant transfer of pastors or change of pulpits in denominational churches doesn't really help the growth of local churches. Allowing a local church pastor to preach one or two Sundays in a month due to too many national programmes or church rotational policy doesn't help the stable growth of the church nor the faith of her members. In a bid to achieve variety through such policy, the church will gradually lose flair for their Pastor.

SUPERNATURAL POWER IN THE LIFE OF THE PASTOR

Grow the pastor, grow the church. The dynamism of the pastor will result in the dynamism of the church. The Church cannot go further than the pastor. The speed of the pastor will always be the speed of the church. Pastors and ministry leaders must have the supernatural power of God in their lives if they hope to gain the confidence of the people.

> *"And the Lord said unto Joshua, this day will I begin to magnify thee in the sight of all Israel, that they may know that, as I was with Moses, so I will be with thee"* (Joshua 3:7).

God's seal of approval must be in the life and ministry of the host pastor, then the people will respect and honour him. Whatever God can do through any guest minister, He must be doing through the host minister. You must prophesy, see vision with your eyes or mouth, preach powerfully, pray for the sick with results and cast out demons. You can't give excuses and still hope to retain people in your church.

Host ministers that are too lazy to rise up to this level will have their churches being overrun by mercenary guest speakers over and over again. Host pastors that abdicate their pastoral

Whatever God can do through any guest minister, He must be doing through the host minister

responsibilities to the people will always struggle with numerical and spiritual growth. Host pastors that are just there to mark time and to welcome various guest speakers to do their job for them will eventually lose the people. Over a one year period, a pastor invited over 28 guest speakers to his church. What an anathema! Small wonder the church is spiritually sick and unstable.

CHAPTER 4

BUILDING THE CHURCH
ON GUEST MINISTERS

A Pastor once invited a friend minister to his church for series of meetings. He comes and goes until he was so conversant with the people. He builds personal relationships with each member by giving them his call cards, phone numbers and personal prayers and prophecies for them. This continued for a while and the Host Pastor was oblivious of what was happening, trusting that his friend cannot sabotage his church.

Well, his trust was misplaced. After another round of meetings in the church by the guest minister, he announced to the church that he wanted to have a special prophetic meeting with some people from a particular tribe of the country. They waited and he had the meeting with them in the absence of the host pastor. Well, he told them at the meeting that 'God' had asked him to start his own church nearby and since they are from his tribe, they should join him in the new church and stop attending the church of someone who is not from their tribe! Before the host pastor could realize what was happening, more than half of his members had moved away with

> *Whenever a guest minister is a super regular face in your church, then you are building the church on him*

this guest minister to form another church few streets away from his. The big mistake here is that the host pastor built the church on that guest minister, consciously or unconsciously.

Whenever a guest minister is a super regular face in your church, then you are building the church on him. Whenever a visiting minister, friend or foe is always regular in almost all your meetings, preaching, praying, counselling and visiting your people, you are building the church on him. Amazingly, quite a number of churches are being run by constantly inviting one guest minister or the other, week in week out.

In many of these churches, people hardly hear the host pastor more than once or twice in a month. Various guest ministers are invited regularly to various weekly or special programmes of the church and they often come with different teachings, controversial interpretations of Scripture and emphasis that leaves you wondering what the host pastor actually stands for. I've seen, heard and witnessed churches that have seven days programmes and they invited seven different speakers. The host pastor hardly preaches, he is only good in doing the announcements and sharing the grace. What a great mistake!

You may ask, why do many pastors build their churches and Ministries on guest ministers? Well, I will answer with the following points:

1.   Lack of knowledge of the work

Many pastors depend only on their secular training, wisdom and knowledge to run the church. They are too busy or proud to go for training and continuous learning so as to be able to handle the complexities of the church of today. And when they are at a loss on what to do, the easiest route is to be inviting one guest minister or the other to fill up for them.

Furthermore, many who are not really called by the Lord but who are too proud to submit under a pastor have gone ahead to start churches and they now employ pastors to lead the church and once they are offended somehow, they fire those unfortunate pastors, only to employ another set of pastors that will later be fired also.

2.   Lack of resourcefulness

Pastors that fail to equip themselves with the word of God and relevant resources that will come handy before and during their ministrations will always depend on guest ministers. Pastors who are gifted as evangelists and prophets are always in this mess. They fail to learn and study, busying themselves only with power ministration and prophetic declarations. Their lack of resources make them to build the church on those guest ministers.

3.   To raise money

Many host ministers are in the habit of using guest ministers to raise money in the church, because their people no longer trust them as a result of misappropriations of past monies. In many situations, guest ministers are invited solely to get money from the people.

Programmes are instituted, not to really bless the people, but to raise money that will be shared by the host pastor and the guest minister. Sometimes, they share it 50/50, 60/40 or 70/30. It depends on how much the guest minister can raise and their agreements. At other instance, he could raise two days offering for the church and one day for himself. In such meetings, offerings are largely hammered on right from the first day. The word of God is of little importance, compared to the offerings. And the success of the meeting is measured, not by the

Pastors that fail to equip themselves with the word of God and relevant resources that will come handy before and during their ministrations will always depend on guest ministers

spiritual blessings that were received by the people, but by how much money was raised by the guest speaker.

While the people go back home spiritually and financially impoverished, the guest speaker and the host pastor smile to the banks! What a mercenary and mercantile spirit! Sadly, this is a practise that has gained ground and is spreading fast among conservative, pentecostal and charismatic churches today. May God save His church and people!

4.   Unfounded fears

Pastors and church founders today are afraid of being monotonous in their message. They are afraid that the people will be tired of hearing them. They therefore invite guest ministers to the church based on that. However, these fears are unfounded. As long as a pastor is fresh, new, relevant and current in his messages and is adequately informed about leading the church, the people will never be tired of hearing him. As long as you are growing and your leadership is meeting the felt and real needs of the people, they will keep coming back to hear you. Guest ministers should only be 'once in a while' affair.

5.   Laziness to go out and learn

A lot of pastors are too lazy to go out and learn better ways of leading the church of today. They detest quality books, tapes, conferences, seminars and trainings that can sharpen their skills as leaders. They depend only on their Bible school training and theological knowledge that cannot meet the basic needs of their people. They are therefore using the same skill, method and strategy, year in, year out; the more reason they depend on guest speakers to run the church for them. Pastors that are too lazy, proud and unwilling to learn from others, to grow, improve and change will always be at the mercy of guest ministers.

Of course, pastors and leaders need helping hand once in a while to build good and well rounded churches, but not to the extent of shifting almost all the burden of ministration to guest ministers. A pastor should be dynamic enough to keep his audience thirsting for more always. Your members must not be tired of hearing you.

ADVERSE EFFECTS OF BUILDING THE CHURCH ON GUEST SPEAKERS

1.   It always result in unstable Christians

When Christians are exposed to scattered preaching, unco-ordinated teachings, and varying emphasis, their faith will be unstable and imbalanced. Shallow and beggarly Christians of today are the direct outcome of this practise.

2.   A scattered church or ministry

Churches and ministries that are built on guest speakers will not really be able to gather their own people. Crowds can come because of the guest speakers, but they will also go away when the guest speakers leave. This is a reality many pastors can attest to. Whenever you have a big name guest speaker in your church or area, crowds of people will come, but after the meetings, you will not find the crowds in the church. Host Pastors need to build themselves in order to gather a following that nobody can take away from them. Churches that are built on guest ministers will always be unstable in membership.

3. Guest ministers sometimes bring strange doctrines and practises to the church

Through prophecies and visions, they do hoodwink people into error and before you know it, many have followed their pernicious ways. For example, guest speaker was invited to a church to preach. He justified divorce, remarriage and separation of couples. Well, the people scattered and went away, even before he finished the sermon, never to gather together again in the church.

4. Domineering ministers

Many churches have been taken over by guest ministers, through spurious miracles, fake prophecies, greediness and covetousness. Many guest ministers have taken over churches and destroyed what it has taken years to build.

A young man related to me on the phone how his 900 members church was scattered through the activities of one guest minister he mistakenly invited. The guest minister came with a strange anointing oil which brought out blood, once it touched people's head. Another pastor wrote me about how he lost his church and wife to a big name guest speaker he invited to minister for him. He lamented that if he had known all these before now, he would not have lost his church and wife.

These and many more are the adverse effects of building churches on guest speakers. On a final note, churches and Church leaders must stop building the church on guest ministers. Rather, the church must be built on the word of God through the host pastor. The foundation and strength of the church must be the undiluted word of God. Host pastors must take time to build and nurture the people in the word, way and will of God consistently.

CHAPTER 5

MERITS AND DEMERITS
OF GUEST MINISTERS

Guest ministers who are true servants of the Lord and are spiritually dynamic can bring blessing, revival and renewal to a church. They can equally bring commotion, chaos, crisis and retrogression to the work if they are ungodly, carnal and money monger.

I was consulting for a big church in Nairobi that had over 150 branches. The man and woman of God over the church were doing a wonderful job for the Lord until they invited a guest minister from Nigeria who prophesied that the Lord wanted them to go into politics and become the president of their country. Unfortunately, they listened to that fake prophecy and today, they have abandoned the ministry and all their attention is now on politics and becoming the next president.

As at the last time I was in Nairobi (March 2007) the annual Pastors' Conference for the church could not hold and I had to return earlier than scheduled. In fact, I had to pay my way back. Why? All their attention is now taken up with political meetings and the church has started to dwindle. I'm afraid the church might go under, unless the Lord intervenes miraculously. All these because of a fake prophecy of a visiting minister.

How can God ask the few labourers in the vineyard to abandon it for another secular pursuit entirely?

To those of you who are politically minded, please answer these questions honestly: How can God ask someone that is doing a great work for the kingdom to abandon it and go and become a politician? What impact does he want to make politically that he cannot make much more spiritually? How can God ask the few labourers in the vineyard to abandon it for another secular pursuit entirely? Has God contradicted himself when He said 'the harvest truly is plenteous but labourers are few' and we should pray for more labourers to reap the already ripened harvest?

There is too much work in the vineyard to allow for secular pursuits. The work needs our total and consistent commitment more than ever before. We must not allow ourselves to be deceived by fake prophecies from Guest Speakers.

PASTORS MYTH ABOUT GUEST MINISTERS

Myths as we all know are half-truths, legends and mindsets that make people to do certain things. In most cases, they are not really truthful, but people believe and operate by them anyway. Many pastors hold some certain myths about guest ministers, the more reason they go after any guest speaker they see or hear about without adequate precaution. They invite just anybody and nasty experiences have been the outcome.

Here are some myths about guest ministers that I've discovered among pastors of various denominations:

Myth 1

Guest Ministers will grow the Church. *'If I can invite a good Guest Speaker, then my Church will grow'*, many pastors usually thought. Pastors with this myth invite every Dick and Harry, Tom and Jerry to their church and still wonder why the church has not really grown. I'm aware of churches where three guest ministers must hold meeting in a month. By the end of the year, they would have welcomed 36 guest ministers, yet the churches didn't fare better, rather they became worse for it, spiritually and financially.

Reality

Though some godly, anointed, God-sent and dynamic guest ministers can be used by God to bring some sputter of numerical and spiritual growth and edification to the church, it is still the host pastor that has the divine responsibility of truly leading the church to durable growth. Guest ministers, no matter how anointed and spiritual they are, can only help and assist the pastor to a certain level. The onus is heavily on the host pastor to buckle up and lead the church to glorious heights. At best, godly guest ministers can lend a helping hand to the Host pastor in the effort to build a growing and glorious church, but the host pastor is responsible for the condition and progress of the church. The work of the best of guest ministers is for a season, while that of the host pastor is for all seasons. Every sincere pastor must jettison this myth and get ready to lead their churches and ministries to durable growth. Develop yourself and become a marketable minister that can draw and magnetise people to your ministry and to the Lord.

Myth 2

Guest Ministers will always draw crowds to the Church. Pastors operating with this mindset spend huge amounts of money to invite popular singers, artists, speakers and ministers to their meetings. They believe that people will be attracted to the church when they hear the names of those popular guest ministers.

Reality 2

The truth of the matter is that even though crowds of people might come as a result of the popular names that were invited to minister in the meetings, research have proven that the crowds don't remain after the popular Speaker finished ministering and departs. Usually, there would be

MERITS AND DEMERITS OF GUEST MINISTERS

overflow of people in the meetings as a result of the popular speaker in attendance. The church is jam-packed every night while his ministration lasted. But as soon as the meeting is over, you won't see the crowds in the church again. What type of work is that?

> *Ninety-five percent of crowds that follow guest speakers to churches usually follow them out too*

Anyway, some money-conscious and greedy pastors are happy with that, since they collect fat offerings during the meetings! But that is not a true work of God, and God will judge such merchantile spirit!

Sustainable growth of the church lies with the dynamism of the Host Pastor, not any big name preacher. God must be at work in the life of the pastor to such an extent that people will be attracted to the church. It is such people that will stay. People that are attracted by the anointing of God upon the pastor and the depth of his character and leadership will usually remain in the church. Ninety-five percent of crowds that follow guest speakers to churches usually follow them out too.

Myth 3

Big name Speakers mean big breakthrough for the Church and Ministry. Pastors with this mindset believe that inviting a big name speaker is tantamount to breakthrough in the church. They are of the opinion that their presence will leave an anointing that will help the church spiritually and financially.

Reality 3

Well, while there is a grain of truth in this myth, yet the reality is far beyond that. A good, godly, anointed and heaven-sent leader can translate the church to the next level through his ministrations, yet the truth is that only God can determine our time and mode of breakthrough. Big name speakers can bring some measure of blessings to the church, but it is the host pastor that will ultimately have to get God's breakthrough for the church.

Realistically, many big name speakers are too busy to bring the true dimension of God to the church. They are too preoccupied with several invitations that their preparation is shallow and fickle. Many of them only have their name to sell and they rely heavily on the past dealings of God in their lives. In most cases, they don't really preach, they always share testimonies of one financial, material and physical blessings that happened years ago and they use that to raise money and pledges for the church.

Many pastors can testify to this truth. God doesn't see the way we see by labelling someone as small or big preacher. I've come to discover that God uses whoever is committed and close to Him. Pastors who have a penchant for big name speakers should think twice. There are many young, dynamic, godly and prayerful ministers that God will use to bring mighty blessings to the church, if given the chance to perform. We need to get divine healing for our craze for big name Speakers.

MERITS FOR GUEST MINISTERS

Guest ministers show good merit when they bring blessing, renewal, restoration and God's power into a church. Guest ministers that keep to their brief, submit under the host minister, keep to time, keep to schedule, preach sound gospel and comport themselves wisely and blamelessly are of good standing and worthy of respect.

> *"Let the elders that rule well be counted worthy of double honour especially they who labour in the word and doctrine"* (I Tim 5:17).

Guest ministers that exemplify humility, lowliness of mind and respect for the host pastor should be honoured again and again. Guest ministers that prove to be a great blessing to the church both by precept and practise should be invited back again on merit. Guest speakers that are open, transparent and honest with the host pastor regarding his dealings, preachings and ministrations in the church should be accorded worthy respect. Guest ministers who stay true to their calling and never meddle with church members nor church politics should be treated with high respect. They should be awarded with the order of merit.

Guest ministers that exemplify humility, lowliness of mind and respect for the host pastor should be honoured again and again

DEMERITS FOR GUEST MINISTERS

However, guest ministers - either local or foreign, that bring strange fire and doctrine to the church, waste people's time through late arrivals and closing, drift off in message to comment on sensitive issues in the church and meddle with church politics should be stopped forthwith. One of such immature Preacher was invited to a church to preach and he started commenting on jewellery or no jewellery, covering or no covering of ladies hair and veered off course entirely. Of course, that was his last time in that church. The pastor had to do a lot of damage control after he left.

I know a guest minister who had no value for time. He usually arrive his venue of ministration two hours late and will also keep the people till very late at night. Since he has refused to change, his invitation to churches and programmes have dwindled drastically. It is only those who don't know him that still invite him. Another preacher was invited to speak at a graduation ceremony. He was given an hour to speak, but he spoke for three hours. All effort to stop him proved abortive, until almost all the invited guests left and nothing tangible was accomplished by the host that day.

Furthermore, guest speakers that are avaricious of money - that charge for ministrations and reject what they are given as too small, should never be invited again. Guest ministers that mess around with women, offering private prayers and prophecy for people should be shamefully driven away and the meetings stopped forthwith.

A guest speaker was in a church for just one week and he slept with some of their women. He deceived them with revelations and fake prophecies. What a shame! Ministers and preachers who in the name of prophecy and deliverance use special objects during ministrations, collect money even when they are not sent, and who are untruthful should not be allowed to minister in the church of Christ.

Guest ministers who lie about their family status, speak from both side of the mouth and are very cunning and crafty with words should not be trusted with our pulpit and church any longer. Such guest ministers are a great demerit to themselves and the church. They only bring crisis, break-away and confusion to the church and shipwreck the faith of people.

> *"But shun profane and vain babblings; for they will increase unto more ungodliness. And their word will eat as doth a canker: of whom is Hymenaeus and Philetus: who concerning the truth have erred, saying that the resurrection is past already; and overthrow the faith of some"* (2 Tim 2:16-18).

The names of such ungodly guest ministers should be published and circulated in churches, just as Apostle Paul did here, so that they can be stopped from doing further damage to people and the body of Christ, or what do you think?

CHAPTER 6

MINISTRY

WITHOUT A BASE

A young man started a ministry some few years back. He claimed to be called by the Lord. Initially, he focused on youth and success, but when the going gets tough, he closed shop and thrives only by welcoming invitation from churches. And when he is not invited, he pesters the pastors through phone calls to invite him to preach and minister in their churches. And that is what he lives by till today. I'm of the high opinion that this is not really the work of God, but a means to keep body and soul together.

Unfortunately, many young men and women are running

this kind of 'Invitation - Driven Ministry' today. They go to churches and ask to be invited to conduct meetings, do vigils, raise money, preach and sing in the church. They usually take a cut from the money they raise and live on that until another invitation will come their way.

Many of them have no office, unattached to any church and have no base you can trace them to. They are too anointed to stay and submit under any leader and all they do is to move from meetings to meetings and seeking for opportunity to preach in any meeting or church. Sometimes, they dress nicely with big Bibles in the hand and visit churches on Sunday morning, requesting to see the pastor. There and then, they demand to preach, claiming the 'Lord' had sent them to the church with special messages and anointing.

Many young men and women are running this kind of 'Invitation - Driven Ministry' today

In many case the unfortunate pastor will oblige them the pulpit and they will grasp such opportunity with both hands to raise money and eat for the next few weeks, until they have opportunity in another church and place. Quite a number of these mobile and freelance speakers have even taken their antics abroad. They will sweet-talk churches and give fantastic testimonies of what they are doing at home which are mostly lies to convince their Hosts to arrange for series of meetings and conferences. They run up hotel bills in the name of their host pastors and collect all the offerings in the meetings and dissappear into thin air. The host church or churches are left to mop up their huge hotel bills and destroyed image.

Reports of incidents of this nature have continually been pouring in from across Africa, not only of what Nigerian ministers have done, but also of what Ghanian, Kenyan, Congolese and South African ministers have done and are doing.

Furthermore, some crooked host pastors have also used these mobile speakers to do some dirty job in their churches. Either they meet on prayer mountains or in another church where they usually strike a bargain with them. They therefore invite them to either raise money, give a particular prophecy, teach some strange doctrines which people have resisted so far or to literally drive some perceived enemies of the pastor out of the church. They repeat the misadventure of Balak king of Moab and Prophet Balaam in Numbers 22:5-6, 10-12;

> *"He sent messengers therefore unto Balaam the son of Beor to Pethor, which is by the river of the land of the children of his people, to call him, saying, Behold, there is a people come out from Egypt: behold, they cover the face of the earth, and they abide over against me: Come now therefore, I pray thee, curse me this people; peradventure I shall prevail, that we may smite them, and that I may drive them out of the land: for I wot that he whom thou blessest is blessed, and he whom thou curset is cursed ...And*

Balaam said unto God, Balak the son of Zippor, king of Moab, hath sent unto me, saying, Behold, there is a people come out of Egypt, which covereth the face of the earth: come now, curse me them; peradventure I shall be able to overcome them, and drive them out. And God said unto Balaam, Thou shalt not go with them; thou shalt not curse the people; for they are blessed.

Since God refused to allow Balaam to go, he devised means and taught Balak what to do, because of money. With the promise of money and gifts, these freelance ministers are ready to do anything in the church. They have no heart for God. All their preoccupation is money, money and money. In a related case some host ministers do take money from foreign guest ministers and allow them to teach strange and devilish doctrines, snap pictures and record videos of their so-called great crusades in Africa that 'saved' millions of souls. These are all business and money making practises that have gained access to the church today.

"For I know this, that after my departing shall grievious wolves enter in among you, not sparing the flock. Also of your own selves shall men arise, speaking perverse things, to draw away disciples after them" (Acts 20:29-30)

"And many shall follow their

pernicious ways, by reason of whom the way of truth shall be evil spoken of. And through covetousness shall they with feigned words make merchandise of you; Whose judgement now of a long time lingereth not, and their damnation slumbereth not" (II Pet. 2:2-3).

They are Preachers,

"Which have forsaken the right way, and gone astray, following the way of Balaam the son of Bosor who loves the wages of unrighteousness" (II Pet. 2:15).

TRUE MINISTRY FROM GOD

Yes, God have not called every one of us to start and lead churches. Surely, God has called some of His children to run ministries that will accelerate the great commission and kingdom expansion. Ministry of evangelism, prophetic, drama, music, youth, children, men, women, writing-literature and prayer-intercession should not necessarily become a church. They can and should be run as para-church ministries that will help the church to become better.

"And say to Archippus, take heed to the ministry which thou hast received in the Lord, that thou fulfil it" (Col. 4:17).

God reserved the right to call anyone into these specialised ministries. Even Timothy that was functioning as the pastor of the church in Corinth had an evangelistic ministry.

> *"But watch thou in all things, endure afflictions, do the work of an evangelist, make full proof of thy ministry"* (II Tim. 4:5).

You can get a copy of my book: **'Fruitful and Fulfilling Ministry Today'** for more information on this. When God calls anyone into any of these ministries, such a person must be patient, watch and allow God to prove Himself on his behalf. If you are under a Leader, you should not just pull away to start your ministry without his approval. If truly God is calling you to start a ministry, let God convince your leader to release you. And anyway, you will always need a covering, mentor, advisor and father in the Lord if the ministry will truly succeed. Don't pull out under your leader without his blessings and prayers. Somehow you 'll need it down the road of life and ministry.

True ministry demands that you must have a base. Not necessarily starting a church, if the Lord is not leading you that way

True ministry demands that you must have a base. Not necessarily starting a church, if the Lord is not leading you that way. But being under a leader or having an office of your own. Don't run a baseless ministry. Have a place you can be traced to. Have a credible Leader as your referee and reference point. Someone you submit to and who knows about you and can vouch for you.

Moreover, don't move about without first proving yourself at home. Prove your call and ministry by reaching out and making impact. Organise meetings and produce resources that will be your reference point. Do something to invite people. Do a solid work that people can relate to and know you for. It is always a mistake to run an 'Invitation-only' ministry, it doesn't really last.

FOR HOST PASTORS

Don't be in a hurry to invite any preacher to your church. Value your pulpit very well and make sure you only give it to those who are credible and worthy. Who you invite to share your pulpit says so much about who you are. People tend to see you in the same light as the one you give your pulpit to, either for good or bad.

A freelance and mobile minister should not step your pulpit except he has a good reference which you have proved to be true. Stand your ground against those who are pestering you with calls for invitation to preach in your church. Whoever you don't know very well and which you have not properly investigated should not be allowed to talk to your people. Take your time to investigate every claim by a preacher and ask questions and be convinced and satisfied before you allow anyone to speak to your people, even if they are few in number. It takes great anointing and hard work to gather the few people! Whoever is not satisfied with your style should go and gather his own audience and see how easy it is!

> *Value your pulpit very well and make sure you only give it to those who are credible and worthy*

Welcoming a guest speaker, who fought with his former leader and has not settled with him, into your church, can and do bring curse to the work. Such a guest speaker is under curse. He first needs to go and settle with his former leader and be prayed for before he can truly be a blessing to your church. Sympatising with an associate that left his leader acrimoniously and giving him your pulpit brings the spirit of rebellion to your people, because you are guilty by association. Let him reconcile with his leader first, then he can be a blessing to the people.

> *"And Nabal answered David's servants, and said, who is David? and who is the son of Jesse? there be many servants now a days that break away every man from his master. Shall I then take my bread, and my water, and my flesh that I have killed for my shearers, and give it unto men, whom I know not whence they be?"* (I Samuel 25:10-11).

CHAPTER 7

EVIL PRACTISES
BY GUEST MINISTERS

T he authority of a popular Pentecostal church in Nigeria had to send a circular to all their local churches about a particular minister that he should never be allowed to minister in their churches again. Why? It was reported and proved to be true that wherever he went to minister as a guest, he had the habit of calling a special vigil for men and there he will ask them to strip naked and masturbate. He collects all their semen and promise to pray specially for them so that they can prosper!

This practise had been going on for years in several churches until he was discovered and banned from preaching in the church. What an occultic and devilish practise by a purported gospel Minister! This is just a tip of the iceberg. Guest ministers have brought incalculable damage to many churches today. In fact, some churches and ministries can hardly recover from the untold damage.

> *"Notwithstanding I have a few things against thee, because thou sufferest that woman Jezebel, which calleth herself a prophetess, to teach and to seduce my servants to commit fornication, and to eat things sacrificed unto idols. And I gave her space to repent of her fornication; and she repented not. Behold, I will cast her into a bed, and them that commit adultery with her into great tribulation, except they repent of their deeds. And I will kill her children with death; and all the churches shall know that I am he which searcheth the reins and hearts: and I will give unto every one of you according to your works"* (Rev. 2:20-23).

As you read this chapter, repent, if you have ever done any of these things I'm going to itemise, as a guest minister. You should be careful of them in your lives and in the life of those you will invite as guests to minister in your church and Ministry.

What are the evil practises of guest ministers? The following are not just unsubstantiated and cooked up stories. They are real, true and from credible sources, that can be vouched for:

1.   Use of occultic power in ministration

This is not strange anymore. The pressure to perform miracles and be highly respected have led many into occultic powers. A guest minister in a church rubs a certain powder on peoples' head and blood will come out in the name of miracles. Well, the over 800 member church scattered as a result and the Pastor had to start all over again.

The pressure to perform miracles and be highly respected have led many into occultic powers

A young pastor invited his mentor to his church to preach. When the mentor came, he was surprised with the crowd that was in the church. Strangely and curiously, after he finished preaching, he removed his shoe and walked out of the church bare-footed. The following week only few people came back to the church. A church of over 500 was reduced to less than 10 due to occultic practise. A preacher I know went to seek for power to grow his church due to the pressure from his wife. He was given the power to bury in his church. In the course of doing this, he became mentally deranged and today the church has closed down and left the city of Lagos.

2.   Sleep with women

This is an all too common practise of guest ministers.

Granted, there are demonic women who want to cause stumbling block to ministers of God, but the rate at which guest ministers are falling through women is becoming alarming. A bishop was preaching in the church of his mentoree. He was lodged in the guest house and four women were assigned to be cooking for him. One afternoon the mentoree decided to pay an unscheduled visit to his mentor, and behold, he met him on top of one of the women. The woman later confessed that she was the one on afternoon duty, while the rest are morning, evening and night duties in that order. What a shame!

A guest minister who was already living in immorality was invited to preach in a church. Through him, the spirit of immorality spread in the church. He not only slept with girls who came to him for counselling, he made sure that boys and girls in the church were sleeping with each other, long after he had gone. That church became a very immoral church and the glory of God departed completely. All because an immoral minister was invited in the first place.

3.   Elope with members

Another evil practise of guest ministers is the act of eloping with rich members of their host churches. Some divorced their wives and marry the women they met in their hosts churches, often times, without the approval and knowledge of their Host Pastor.

A bishop friend of mine in South Africa told me the story of the guest minister he once invited to his church. This preacher preached wonderfully well. But unknown to my friend, he was already chasing after one of the ladies in the church. After he was gone, the lady was found missing too. It was later discovered that he eloped with her. After much effort, the lady came back to the church few months later, but she died two months later! A guest minister in a church in Lagos also eloped with the wife of a brother in the church. She was brought back after law enforcement agents were unleashed on the preacher.

4. Start their own church from host's members

Many guest ministers have started their own churches with the members of their host's church. They use prophecy, miracles and craftiness to draw disciples after themselves. Few weeks later after visiting a church, their church will spring up nearby with the members of their host's church forming the nucleus.

A guest minister who was invited from abroad was fascinated by the gifts and money he was given by his host the first time. When he was invited the second time, he had perfected plan to start his own church, so that he can have all such money unto himself. He instigated the members against the host pastor and went away with them to start. But the church only lasted for six months. Why? His motive was wrong, his method ungodly and his foundation shaky. His host had to lick his wounds and started all over again.

5. Raise money through foul means

The basic motive of most guest ministers of today is money. Edifying the body of Christ and expanding God's kingdom takes the back burner in their hearts. They are therefore ready to get money through crooked means. A guest speaker

Guest speakers today raise offering for themselves and demand how much they will be paid.

came to a church with three kinds of cards that can purportedly turn people to millionaires. The three are labelled as gold, silver and bronze. You must buy which ever you choose with thousands of Naira and then you will be given another card that will be generating money for you in your house. People paid thousands to purchase the cards and he went away smiling. Of course, nobody became a millionaire!

In a city-wide meeting in Jos Nigeria some few years ago, a preacher told the people that if anyone will give him ten thousand Naira, God will buy a luxurious bus for the person by December of that year. Trust our *Igbo* people, they came with N10,000 each in their hundreds. The preacher went away with the money and not a single person bought a luxurious bus by December of that year or later years. Till he died two years ago, that preacher cannot step into the city of Jos again. Guest speakers today raise offering for themselves and demand how much they will be paid. These are thieves and robbers in the temple.

6.   Fake miracles and gifts of the Spirit.

In order to garner respect and be seen as one with the great power of God, many guest ministers use fake anointing oil to push people down, perform fake miracles and give false prophecies. Sometimes, they use psychology to discern the needs of people and touch them. But the truth is that the problem of the people usually persist or at best they get temporary relief, but the problems usually come back double or triple fold later.

A guest minister uses a particular anointing oil to rub his hands before each ministration and everyone he spreads that hand to must fall down. Another preacher's wife was searching the pocket of the suits of her husband in preparation for taking them to the dry cleaner. She found a 'juju' in one of the pockets. She reported this to her husband's mentor and to her surprise the mentor merely waved it off saying "you need those things to perform miracles so that people can come to church and the gospel can be preached to them" It's amazing that God now needs the devil's help to win souls!

A popular guest speaker in a church usually comes to the meeting very early. He will stay in the car park to meet with people and interview them. Surprisingly when he begins his ministration, the 'word of knowledge' from him is only directed at those sitting in the front and whom he had met earlier in the car park. What a trick and crafty way to deceive people! Of course, nothing will really happen in the life of the people. The meeting was eventually cancelled by the host pastor when this was discovered. But by then, he had raked in thousands of dollars.

7. **False testimonies to attract giving from people**

Many guest ministers embellish the truth and exaggerate events so as to hoodwink people. Many times, they tell outright and blatant lies so as to make people give to them. Some of them will give a large amount in the presence of people, but will later collect it back after the meeting!

A popular guest speaker gives a fantastic testimony of how he sowed his car to another pastor and two weeks later, God blessed him with a 4 X 4 Jeep. He also talked about a pledge he made to a church to buy all their chairs and God blessed him mightily in return. Unknown to him, another senior minister that knew the true position of thing and about those testimonies was in the audience. After the meeting, he was confronted and he was profuse with apology. He said he was trying to motivate the people to give. What a false pretense! No wonder, people gave and gave, yet they became poorer and poorer. Most prosperity preachings only profit the preachers, not the people and the kingdom of God!

8. Take advantage of platform to fester their own nests

Most guest speakers are ingrates. They don't really appreciate the opportunity and platform given them by their host ministers. All they are concerned with is how to take advantage of such platform to start their own ministry or school and create a following. Most guest speakers have become opportunists. They distribute their call cards, phone numbers and contacts details. They meet privately with members and go behind their hosts to meet with these people. You only get to hear when things go wrong.

I've experienced much of this in our ministry. I've brought fellow ministers to lecture in our school and conferences, only for them to use the platform to start their own school, draw our students to their schools and discourage them from coming to our conferences. One even wrote at the front of his seminar paper that was sold in one of our conferences: 'contact me for mentoring and ministration.' Haba! That is sheer opportunism!

I know of preachers who were invited to countries to minister and they create schism in the body of ministers there so that they can start their own ministerial body that will be subject to their whims and caprises. And they will later boast that they have ministers under them in every country of the world'. How did they gather them? Through crook and deceit!

9. Instigate associates against their pastors

Some of the breakaways in churches were instigated by guest speakers. They do that by giving false prophecies to the associates or they share false vision that their senior pastors are using their 'stars' to prosper in the church. 'The Lord had therefore said they should move away to start their own'. With sweet words, they deceive gullible and innocent souls and before you know it, the church begins to experience crisis.

A guest speaker did exactly like this in a church, and the once humble and faithful associate began to find fault with his leader, until he went away suddenly. By the time he realised his error, it was too late to return because he had severely bitten the finger that fed him. Quite sadly such guest speakers have nothing more to

> *Some of the breakaways in churches were instigated by guest speakers*

offer those deceived souls when the going gets tough.

10 Scatter churches, destroy homes and create bad image

Many churches have been scattered by too many guest speakers and many homes have been destroyed due to fake prophecies. In a church, the guest minister picked a woman as a witch, though the prophecy was false, yet the husband divorced her and the home broke down irretrievably due to the seed that was sown by the fake guest speaker. A guest minister was invited to a church and he brought all his past occultic paraphernalia for display. Occultic drums were displayed in the church. The outcome? More than five people died in the church in an accident and the leader of the church had a broken arm, leg and head few weeks later.

HOW TO STEM THESE PRACTISES

More examples could be cited, but suffice with all these. A concerned and discerning person will ask, why do we allow all these to happen in the church and against the church? I believe that blind trust by pastors have contributed a lot in this direction. Blind trust and failure to scrutinise, properly and patiently investigate whom we want to

Blind trust and failure to scrutinise, properly and patiently investigate whom we want to invite have allowed many guest speakers to have a field day

invite have allowed many guest speakers to have a field day. Blind trust that doesn't make the host pastor to carefully watch and monitor their guest speakers have contributed in no small measure to all these malaise. Blind trust that will not believe early warning signals of a guest speaker gone awry have helped all these ungodly scenarios.

How can we identify these kinds of guest speakers? Always look for tell tale signs that you have read in this book and once you see one or two, don't hesitate to take drastic action. How can we stop them? By prayer, church embargo on them and putting them to ridicule. Their names and doings must be spread to other churches to serve as deterrent.

CHAPTER 8

HOW TO COMPORT YOURSELF

AS A GUEST MINISTER

A veteran preacher was hosted by a church for one week indoor meeting. He was very difficult to handle. He complained about almost everything. He placed high demands on the church, though he preaches very well, yet he was not keeping to time and he had a very large appetite. He finishes a medium size chocolate drink of *Bournvita* in two days. At the end of one week, the church was in debt because of his unreasonable demands. He even rejected the honorarium he was given as too small and demanded that much more should be added. Well, the church promised never to invite him or his likes again.

Very many guest ministers, even though some of them had been in the ministry for long, don't know how to comport or behave themselves in a blameless way today. Even though this preacher is a veteran in the ministry, yet he had not learnt proper and dignified behaviour that should epitomise guest ministers. He failed to follow the example of Apostle Paul among the Thessalonian Christians;

> *Wittingly and unwittingly, many guest ministers have become stumbling blocks to the faith of many people and churches by their wrong conducts.*

> *"Ye are witnessess, and God also, how holily and justly and unblameably we behaved ourselves among you that believe"* (I Thess. 2:10).

Apostle Paul made sure that he was a good example to those Christians in all his conduct and manners. Wittingly and unwittingly, many guest ministers have become stumbling blocks to the faith of many people and churches by their wrong conducts.

Like all the evil behaviours that were enumerated in the last chapter, the faith of many of such victims have been destroyed and they have backslidden. It will only take the grace and mighty work of the Holy Spirit to bring them back to the Lord. A fearful judgement awaits preachers who are destroying churches and faith of others by their ungodly and unethical practises.

Hear what Luke 17:1-2 says regarding this:

> *"Then said he unto the disciples, it is impossible but that offences will come; but woe unto him, through whom they come! It were better for him that a millstone were hanged about his neck and be cast into the sea, than that he should offend one of these little ones".*

The church is the most important property of God on earth. He will therefore not take kindly to anyone that is bringing crisis, chaos and disintegration to that church. God will deal with such one and visit him with wrath. Apostle Paul knew the place of the church in the heart of God and therefore wrote young Timothty about how he should comport himself therein.

> *"But if I tarry long, that thou mayest know how thou oughest to behave thyself in the house of God,which is the church of the living God, the pillar and ground of the truth".* (I Tim 3:15).

There are right ways to behave and wrong ways to behave in the church, both by members, leaders and guest ministers. In order to help those who are sincere and searching, I will enumerate proper ways to behave as a guest minister. I will write from my own experience and that of others also.

As I'm writing, I'm a guest minister in a house in Paris, France, and ministering in the churches in the evenings. My ministry takes me round a lot. This year alone(2007), I have been to over five countries by June and many cities in Nigeria. Sometimes I'm kept in a house or lodged in a hotel. The following conducts are what I've used as guidelines and God has helped me to have good testimonies in every place he had opened doors for our ministry.

1.   Be clear on your purpose of invitation.

Know why you are invited and what you are invited to do and accomplish through your message or prayers. Seek for clarifications from your hosts. Don't just go anywhere without an aim and a clear purpose.

2.   Seek for the leading of the Lord.

Pray and get God's assurance to go or not to go. You don't have to honour every invitation. If truly it is God's work and you are his servant, know His mind about your honouring that invitation or not. I know of preachers that didn't wait to get the mind of God about invitations and they went and contacted what destroyed them spiritually in such meetings.

3.   Pray and prepare much

Once you get the green light from God to go, start to pray and prepare yourself. Seek the face of the Lord for strength, power, wisdom and anointing that will make your ministration to have mighty spiritual impact in the life of the church, ministry or people. Every ministration must leave a lasting impact and impression on the people and intensive prayers from you will make that possible.

4. Stand up, speak up and shut up

Preach Jesus and nothing more. Lift Jesus up, not yourself. Preach the gospel, not doctrines and ideas of men. Start in time and close in time. Don't be a long winded speaker that takes up much time of the people. In your preaching, stay within your brief and stay in the word of God. Avoid controversial topics and ideologies. Be a true servant of the Lord and close when they still have a good taste in their mouth. Preach your heart out. Stop being a professional preacher but a true servant of the Lord.

5. Be time conscious

Make it a habit to keep to time. Arrive in time, don't keep your host in anxiety- waiting for you. Be a man of time. Ask for the time allotted to your ministration and keep to it. Sometimes, you are given 20, 30, 40, 45 minutes or an hour to speak. By all means, keep to the time you are given. Rather close before your time than out-shoot the time.

> *Preach Jesus and nothing more. Lift Jesus up, not yourself. Preach the gospel, not doctrines and ideas of men.*

Cut back your message and emphasise the most important points. There is no law that says you should finish all you prepared. Wasting the time of people reduces your honour and closes door against you.

6. Submit under your host pastor

Once you agree to come and minister in a church, you are automatically under the authority of the host pastor. Don't behave as if you are above him or know more than him. Be humble and submissive to the briefing you are given. You must abide by the order of the house. You can't do what you like in a place where you are invited. Even if you are the mentor of your host, you must submit to him, once you are ministering in his church. If he asked you not to raise money, you must obey, no matter how strongly you feel. Honour your host in word and deed and his people will love you. Comments such as 'your pastor is my boy'; 'I gave him the Holy Spirit inside of him', should be jettisoned, they only lower your respect with the people. Remember, you are not in your church but his church and respect is reciprocal. Never undermine your host in whatever form. Garner support for your host through your ministrations.

7. Live what you preach

Be a true example of godliness. By word and deeds, show that you are real and genuine. Let your life and living be in consonance with the word of God. Be a model of righteousness and genuine christian life. Know that you are being watched, so, be careful the way you live. If you don't have it, you can't give it to them. If your life is at variance with the word you preach, it will show sooner or later. One good example is worth more than a thousand sermons. Your living is what will give power to your words. A hypocrite preacher will lose the confidence and respect of people, sooner or later.

8. Stay where you lodged

If you are lodged by the church, either in a house or hotel, make sure you stay there. Stop moving about town or going to the house of members without the knowledge of your host. Stay where you are lodged and spend your time praying, reading, studying and resting for your meetings. If you are the restless type, then discipline yourself to rest and stay where you are kept. It is unbecoming for a preacher to get lost in town or be found in another place other than where you are kept. Keep the place clean, neat and tidy. Be clean and neat yourself. Don't destroy the properties left in your care and in your room.

> *It is wrong for guest ministers to make contact with the members of their host's church in his absence*

9. Place no demand on your host

Don't place unnecessary demand for money, clothings, food, favourite dish or particular delicacies on your host. Don't be too hard to please. It is unethical for a preacher to be a slave of food and become gluttonous. Take what you are given. Be open to eat whatever is available. As a missionary and servant of the Lord, you must not run the church into debt in their effort to satisfy your heavy appetite. Be disciplined in your eating. Even when the church gives you free ticket to eat anything you like, still demonstrate discipline and godly consideration.

10. Don't make solicited or unsolicited contact with members.

It is wrong for guest ministers to make contact with the members of their host's church in his absence. It is wrong to distribute your contact details to those you meet in your host's church. Meeting them one by one after the meeting and giving out your telephone numbers and going to visit them without the knowledge of your host is absolutely wrong and unethical. It leads to quarrel and bad blood among Ministers. Be open and transparent with your host. If they give you gifts, show it to your host. If someone you meet in your host's church wants to invite you to his office, house or church, let your host know from the onset and seek his consent. In fact, let him be the one to introduce you and work out your connection. That is the ethical thing to do. Though many are neck deep in this unethical practises, yet that doesn't mean it's right to do it.

11. Don't be an opportunist

It is godly and ethical to appreciate the platform given to you by your host to share with his people. Show deep gratitude for it and don't you ever abuse that platform. Take it as a service to the Lord and comport yourself wisely. Don't take advantage of that platform to fester your own nests by undermining the influence and ministry of your host. Don't start any work near your host's church. Don't run a parallel ministry, neither should you welcome complaints and rumours about him. Don't be jealous and envious of your host's success that you have to do stupid and foolish things such as instigating his Associates against him and hearing false accusations against him.

Comments such as 'If I were your pastor' must never find its way into your mouth. Don't distribute the programme of your church or of your ministry in your host's church and meetings without his approval. In fact, the ethical thing to do is to let him do the announcements by himself, if he so wishes. Undermining your host in anyway is undermining yourself and any ministry you build on that behaviour will never last.

12.   Stay clear of the opposite sex

If your host request for your wife, bring her along. If not, don't come with another woman. It is unethical to travel to ministrations where you are going to be lodged with another woman that is not your wife. Many preachers go with their personal assistants or worship leader of the opposite sex and the two of them will stay in the same room. That is ungodly, unethical and controversial. Many have fallen and divorced their wives as a result of this. Come alone, if you can't come with your wife or at best come with another male companion.

In your host's church, converse sparingly with women and never counsel them alone in privacy. Many church members love guest ministers and they will flock to you *enmasse*, but you must be careful. Let your host know immediately all they

> *It is unethical to travel to ministrations where you are going to be lodged with another woman that is not your wife*

told you or are telling you. Don't give counseling appointment in your room or hotel to a lady. Even if you did nothing with her, it will generate suspicion and controversy that will take long time to heal and cause crisis of confidence in the church. Be open, clean and clear in your dealings with your Host Pastor. Stay away from accusations of sexual harassments

13. Don't meddle with church politics

Of course, some members or church elders will make attempt to report their pastor to you. They would want to air their grievances in your ears and wants your sympathy. Don't give room for that. Don't be the garbage can where they can dump all their displeasure with the leadership of the church. Encourage them to go humbly to their pastor and settle their differences. At best, use your preaching to whip up support and cooperation with the pastor. You are there to help build the church, not to scatter or cause disaffection. Do your assigned task and get out of the picture. Get out of that church and stay out until you are probably invited again.

14. Don't give your personal opinion, unless it is solicited for

You may see many things that are wrong and needed attention in the church, but don't say anything or air your views unless they pointedly asked you. It is foolish to give your opinion when nobody asks nor need it. Keep your mouth shut and pray for the church. But if they ask for your candid assessment of the church, then you can speak forthrightly and clearly.

15. Take whatever you are given.

If at the end of your ministration, you were given gifts, money and treasures, take it, no matter how big or small they are, because the labourer is worthy of his wages. Stop rejecting gifts, except the Lord asked you to, neither should you be angry at the smallness or littleness of it. Receive them with

> *It is absolutely wrong and immoral to charge for ministrations in a church or ministry related events*

thanksgiving. At other times, you are not given anything, thank the Lord and move away. Stop getting annoyed in such instances. I've been to places where I was given nothing after days and hours of ministration. I've been at other places where I was given little. I've also been at places where I was given money and gifts beyond my expectation and widest imagination. In it all, I've come to discover this truth: God is the one that pays the wages of His servants. No man can pay the servant of the Lord. It is only God that does that and He does it in variety of ways, least expected by you.

It is absolutely wrong and immoral to charge for ministrations in a church or ministry related events. It is equally wrong to have money as the motive when going for ministrations. Those who do these are mercenaries and not servants of the Lord. It is also wrong to reject invitations simply because no good money will come out of it.

In some instances, you get to a church and they give you

money and the Lord asked you to return it to them or sow it to that struggling church or work. That has happened to me in many places. You just have to obey, if you are a true servant of the Lord. If money is your reason of being in the ministry, you've missed your way long ago. If money is your motive of ministrations, God might have left you long ago, unknown to you. The footsteps of God that you are still hearing at your back is not the footsteps of God walking towards you, but the footsteps of God walking away!

16.   Don't be angry at simple introductions

Amazingly, there are many preachers who get annoyed when they are simply introduced to the church. They feel peeved that all their titles, names, achievements and acquirements were not mentioned in the introduction. They change colour and become sad and angry with the host pastor. Others feel that the person that was given the task of introducing them is below them and therefore did not do a good job. One speaker even had to re-introduce himself when he was given the microphone. Another Speaker had to mention all his titles, talk about his cars and mansion that was just constructed, which were not mentioned in the introduction. A popular preacher in Lagos got really angry with a host pastor that failed to equally introduce his wife and accord her great honour. He said his host had 'committed an unpardonable sin'. Haba! Because of mere introduction? How proud and self centered we can be as preachers!

If you are really a servant of the Lord and you have a heart to serve the Lord and His church, you'll be okay with simple introduction and let the Lord prove himself in your life.

There are preachers who are greatly and loudly introduced to the church, but their ministrations were shallow, carnal and of little benefit to the people.

Nearly all the time, this is the case with preachers who take delight in the hype and adulation of men. But there are humble servants of the Lord, whose only motive is to glorify the Lord and be a blessing to the people, that were simply introduced and yet, the Lord glorified himself in their ministrations and the church was mightily edified. This humble approach should be our method. Whatever you have achieved in the past is by the grace of God, so all the glory should go to Him. Throwing your weight around and displaying insecurity through extravagant introductions should be jettisoned from our lives and scheme of doing things, if really we are humble servants of the Lord.

If you can adopt, adapt, adjust and be guided by these practical ways of comporting yourself as a guest minister, then God will be with you in earnest and the church of Christ will become better through you.

CHAPTER 9

HOW TO HANDLE
GUEST MINISTERS

Many young ministers are at a loss on how to handle guest ministers. In this chapter, I want to pinpoint codes of conduct that relates to inviting and handling of guest ministers. Codes are general and moral guidelines of respected professions. Every guest minister and host pastors must know and relate by these code of conducts.

* Proper prayer and seeking of God's face before contacting him. Don't contact a preacher you have not seriously prayed about.

* Proper contact and agreement must be done and

he must agree before you start your publicity. It is immoral to start using the name of a speaker in your publicity when you have not contacted him. Many do it, but it's wrong.

* Clear purpose and message must be stated in the invitation letter. Be clear on your purpose of inviting him to come and minister. State it in black and white.

* Let him know the order of the house as to when to start, what to do and what not to do, plus when to stop. Don't be too humble to state these.

* Invite only the guest speakers you know very well or you have a good report about and that leaders can vouch for his genuineness.

* Don't ever invite big names and garrulous ministers you'll not be able to handle. Many young pastors have lost their ministry as a result of inviting a big names speaker that they cannot handle.

* Don't ever invite a guest minister when you are not going to be around in the church, no matter how close you are to him. Doing so is an invitation to disaster.

* Find a standard guest house or hotel for ministers outside your locality. If you are not ready to take care of your invited guest very well, don't invite him.

* Your protocol officers of the same sex must take good care of him. There have been many cases of

protocol officers that elope with guest ministers.

* You must meet with him when he arrives and share fellowship together as a mark of respect and honour.

* Be around to monitor and assess the guest minister during his ministrations. Don't be too busy running around that you don't have time to listen to the ministration of your Guest.

* Don't hand over the church to a guest minister to do as he pleases or as the 'Lord' leads him. Blind trust leads to scandals and crisis.

* Guest speakers that are controversial and preach errors or church dogmas should be stopped forthwith. Don't be too humble to correct errors you see in guest ministers immediately. Be bold and wise to correct Scriptural errors before dismissing the service. Don't wait for another day. It must be done immediately before he leaves.

* Introduce him to the church simply and truthfully - no embellishments. Let him prove himself in his ministrations.

* Prepare the honorarium of your guest speaker well in advance and be generous to him. Ask the members to bless him also with gifts.

* Demand that issues, visions, prophetic words and revelations must be clarified with you before it is released to the congregation.

* Guest ministers that are too proud to obey the leadership of the host pastor should be sent away immediately and the meeting cancelled.

* Guest ministers that raised money for themselves publicly or privately should be stopped there and then.

* Guest speakers that are discovered to be fake, liars and immoral must be driven away immediately and the meeting taken over by the host pastor.

* Guest ministers offering private prophecies and prayers to people should be stopped forthwith.

* Guest ministers that are begging to be invited either have ulterior motive or are only after money. Don't ever invite them.

* Boldly confront and denounce a guest minister that broke ethical standards and descend low to do evil things. Watch your hand and that of the Ccurch clean from such practise.

* Guest ministers that charge for ministrations or that demand for percentage of the offerings should be sent away immediately. They will not do you nor the church any good on the long run.

* Guest ministers that have no base with a credible organisation should not be invited. Once you are not clear in your spirit, even if he has arrived, send him

back with his honorarium, but don't allow him to lead your people. This may be tough, but it is the right thing to do, if you really value your work and people.

* Guest ministers that bring strange objects, occultic paraphernalia and special anointing oil to help their ministrations must never be allowed in the church.

Guest ministers must be blessings to the church and not sources of curse. Those who bring problems and crisis to the church will be judged by the Lord.

CHAPTER 10

HOW TO REMUNERATE
GUEST MINISTERS

Throughout this book, I have written against mercenaries and merchantile spirit in guest ministers. In my preachings and teachings, I do the same. I'm strongly convinced that God is the one that pays the wages of His servants. However, I need to strike a good balance with this chapter.

The Scripture is clear that ministers should be remunerated. Jesus says that 'the workman is worthy of his meat' (Matt 10:10).

"And in the same house remain, eating and drinking such things as

they give; for the labourer is worthy of his hire. Go not from house to house"
(Luke 10:7).

I'm sorry to report that many fundamental, conservative and holiness churches today have not taken these scriptures to heart. They invite ministers but they don't remunerate them. They do everything and prepare very well for a programme but they will not prepare well the honorarium of the speaker.

In many instances, they only try to raise offering and package something very small after the speaker has finished and he is ready to leave. I've been a victim of this very many times. In some other cases, they promise to send your honorarium few days later, but you'll never receive anything years later. Sometimes, the person that was sent used it without getting to you nor reporting back to the church. This has also happened to me.

"For it is written in the law of Moses, thou shalt not muzzle the mouth of the ox that treadeth out the corn. Doth God take care for the oxen? Or saith he it altogether for our sakes? For our sakes, no doubt, this is written: that he that ploweth should plow in hope, and that he that thresheth in hope should be partaker of his hope ... Do ye not know that they which minister about holy things live of the things of the temple? and they which wait at the altar are partakers with the altar?

Even so hath the Lord ordained that they which preach the gospel should live of the gospel" (1 Cor. 9:9-10, 13-14).

In the light of this revealing scriptural passage, we can deduce that churches that shortchange ministers are displeasing unto the Lord. Churches that use ministers without appreciating them financially or otherwise are only stealing from themselves. Churches that invite ministers to come without being responsible for their upkeep, transport and some take home, are bringing curses upon themselves.

I've even personally experienced cases where the church asked the people to sow into the life of the guest minister and an offering was taken yet the money was never given or only a fraction of it is given to the guest minister. What a way of bringing curse and God's wrath upon a church and a ministry!

Many churches are neck deep in this problem. I know of ministers that have been extensively used by the churches and yet they were given next to nothing and today they are old and forgotten. What a wicked way to repay sincere and genuine men of God. It is this selfish and stingy attitude by the majority of the church that has led many young ministers to start charging for ministrations and to devise means of getting money from the churches. Though that is

> **Churches that use ministers without appreciating them financially or otherwise are only stealing from themselves**

an extreme reaction that is condemnable and unethical.

HOW TO REMUNERATE GUEST MINISTERS

Do your home work very well before you venture to invite a guest minister. If you don't have anything to give, be open to him and let him decide whether to come or not. If what you have is little and small, let him know from the onset. Very many guest ministers will surely appreciate this kind of frankness from host pastors. In a number of occasions, I've been to churches where I had to even sow to their needs and bless them so that they can grow and come up. I've been to countries where I paid for my ticket, my hotel, my food, my transport and even fed the pastors in the effort to reach them and help the kingdom of God to grow and expand.

Whenever we want to bring a guest minister to our meetings and church, either from close or far away places, these are good rules to follow in remunerating him.

* Prepare well his honorarium in advance
* Raise the honorarium through members or church purse
* Consider the distance and cost of his coming.
* Be generous and open handed.
* Provide refreshments before, during and after his ministrations.
* Bless him very well that he'll be happy to come back again.
* Ask and train your members to also give gifts to your guests.

* You can raise special seeds that must be given to him without you counting it.
* Your gifts can be in kind or in cash.
* If he had travelled from far, you must pay his ticket, transport, hotel, feeding and give him a cup of water in appreciation.
* You can raise a partners forum that have the duty of raising seeds for your guest speakers.

When guest ministers are well remunerated, they will bless the church from the depth of their hearts and the church will be truly blessed.

> *"For whosoever shall give you a cup of water to drink in my name, because ye belong to Christ, verily I say unto you, he shall not lose his reward"* (Mark 9:41).

Make it a policy that nobody ministers in your church and go empty handed. Even those who only come to visit your church must go home with transport fare.

CHAPTER 11

PROTOCOL PRACTISES

FOR GUEST MINISTERS

Having gone round hundreds of churches all over Nigeria, across Africa and the world, I feel I can speak authoritatively on the issue of protocol. I have seen protocol being practised in basically two ways in the various churches.

Protocol can be described as the act of welcoming, guiding and caring for our guests and making their stay and time with us as enjoyable and hassle free as much as possible. Usually, it is a department in the church, headed oftentimes by the personal assistant to the pastor or by the Host minister himself.

Often times, the level of protocol of a church is subject to the exposure of the host pastor himself. If he is localized and unexposed, he will handle it very poorly. On the other hand, if the host pastor is well exposed and informed, he will have a vibrant and responsive protocol department.

Now, coming back to the two ways I mentioned earlier, churches practise protocol in two extreme ways. The first extreme is a situation where there is virtually no protocol for Invited guests. They are invited through phone or SMS and no personal contact was made and if the guest decides to come anyway, nobody will be there to welcome him. No information given to him, no preparation done, no place to stay and he is badly treated in such a way as to tell him that they are doing him a favour by inviting him. I have been a victim of such treatment in a number of ocassion.

> *The level of protocol of a church is subject to the exposure of the host pastor himself*

The second extreme is the extravagant protocol practises of Charismatic and Pentecostal churches. The guest is treated like a President of a country. Protocol officers swarm around him, expensive 4 X 4 cars are rented to carry him around. Expensive hotel suits are lavishly paid for, first class airline tickets are provided and hefty men are contacted to provide the 'man of God' with security. He is kept away from the people and he can only come to the church during his ministrations and he must leave immediately he finishes his message. I've also tasted this.

I'm aware that some guest speakers demand for all these and many more before they can be invited to a church! Well, are we no longer servants of the Lord? Undoubtedly, these things bring pride to the human heart and many of those practising it are being forsaken by the Lord. Such sheer waste of money in the name of honour and respect will not be condoned by the Lord for too long. Missions, church planting, social service to the poor and needy will be better off with these monies that are being flagrantly wasted. My determination is to strike a balance between these two extremes through this chapter. Now here we go:

A. Have a functional protocol department in the church.

Your protocol department must be up and running whenever you are to host a guest minister. The volunteer officers must be truly saved, sanctified and well trained and contented. They must be people that have flair for communication and well mannered. The impression they create go a long way to describe your church.

b. Budget for your guests.

Before you venture to invite a guest minister, check your budget. How much do you have to spend on your guest? What can you afford? How much will be for hotel, food and transport? How much honorarium can you give him? After you decide all these, then set about how to raise the budget. Don't invite the guest minister if you can not raise the budget before hand. It is manipulative to use him to raise your budget. If really the Lord wants you to hold the meetings and to invite that particular guest minister, then

He will provide for your needs ahead of time.

c. Protocol officers of the same sex must be handy to welcome your Guests.

If you are inviting a male guest, your officers must be males. If a female, the same females must welcome her. They should have information about his/her movement and be there on time to provide quality and godly service to your guest.

d. Host pastors must meet with their guests before the service

Don't be too busy not to meet with your guest before the meeting starts, especially if he is coming to your church for the first time. It is a mark of disrespect and careless attitude when you only meet your guest in the hall of meeting for the first time. It doesn't portray you in good light.

E. Provide a good hotel for him

Even if he is staying for one night, get him a place that is suitable, private and restful for him. Let him be able to have a good night rest. This place must have been secured beforehand. It does not necessarily have to be a very expensive place.

f. Provide good food for him

Your guest must not go hungry. If he decides to fast, then that's his choice. It should not be because food is unavailable. Good drinks, juices and refreshments must be provided and handy at all times.

G.   Provide a good car, if he didn't come with any

As much as God helps you, provide a good car to take your guest around. Not necessarily an expensive one, but a functional car. If he doesn't come with any, you can arrange to be taking him home every night, provided he is from the same city or place.

h.   Ask for his taste and try to meet it

It is good and thoughtful to ask for the taste of your guest in food and drink and try within your power to meet it. But don't run into debt doing that.

i.   He should not only come to preach and go

I've seen this in practise very much. Preachers only come to the church few minutes to their sermon time and once they finish, they are driven away. In some cases, this might be justified, but generally speaking, it doesn't help the Preacher nor the church.

Guest ministers should partake in the worship service and have a feel of

Whisking preachers off immediately after his sermon and bringing him around few minutes to his ministration engenders pride in him and disallows him to have a true feel of the meeting

the church. He too should be a worshipper. He should be in the service with the people. Peradventure, God will change his message and give him a special word for the church. God can also bless the guest through the ministrations and words he will hear during the worship. If he feels he wants to stay around to listen to other speakers, he should be allowed and enjoy the fellowship of the brethren. Whisking preachers off immediately after his sermon and bringing him around few minutes to his ministration engenders pride in him and disallows him to have a true feel of the meeting.

j.   Keep to time of meeting and appointment

Good protocol practises demand that time of meeting must be strictly followed. It is wrong to keep your guests waiting endlessly. Start the meeting in time and late comers will meet you along the way.

k.   Appreciate him and warmly send him away

Let his honorarium be ready and give it to him once he finished. Thank him warmly and release him to go. Some churches have the practise of coming back some few days later to give whatever they have to their guest minister. If that is your preference, don't let it be too long. Do it in time and get on with other things.

Conclusively, allowing your guest to have interaction with your people is at your own discretion and the purpose of which you call him for. If it's a teaching, prophetic and deliverance meetings, there is no way they will not need clarifications through questions and answers, personal ministrations and touch. But if it's only a preaching conference or Sunday service, then your guest can go away without any interaction with your audience.

In all things, you must show wisdom, tact, respect and love to your guests at all times

In all things, you must show wisdom, tact, respect and love to your guests at all times. If you suspect anything, be bold and courageous enough to take it up with him and hear his own side. Settle whatever differences and march on with your Ministry. Whoever you are not really free with, should not be invited to your church. Stop inviting the preacher you cannot trust.

I believe that if churches should practise their protocols along these lines, things will generally be okay. Any little problems here and there can be quickly nipped in the bud.

Finally,
> *"Let love be without dissimulation. Abhor that which is evil: cleave to that which is good. Be kindly affectioned one to another with brotherly love; In honour preferring one another"* (Romans 12:9-10).

CHAPTER 12

OF GUEST

MUSICIANS AND PROPHETS

Over the last few years there have been major transformations in the music departments of most churches. I'm sorry to say that majority of these transformations are not positive, but very negative in nature. Christian music have moved from being a source of ministration, comfort and edification of souls to mere entertainment and professional performance. The lyrics have changed, the beat has become faster, the wordings are no longer clear and the power is gone. Even when the sacred songs and hymnals are being sang, the life and meaning is no longer there.

Very many people that started from church choir and professed to know the Lord have now become professional artists. organists, keyboardists, instrumentalists and Singers have all gone with the change that have been witnessed in the music industry.

Christian music have moved from being a source of ministration, comfort and edification of souls to mere entertainment and professional performance

They have all displayed the following traits:
* Most of them live wayward lives.
* Most of them don't know the Lord.
* Many have lost their relationship with God.
* Most don't know the will and way of the Lord.
* They now sing to entertain, not to minister.
* They now charge for services and performance.
* They copy worldly songs and systems.
* They sing for money and ephemeral things.

The power and Spirit of God is gone from most of these professional performers. No conversion, no spirituality nor deliverance of the soul from clutches of Satan when they sing. But when David sang and played instruments, king Saul was delivered from evil spirits.

"And it came to pass, when the evil spirit from God was upon Saul, that

David took an harp, and played with his hand; so Saul was refreshed, and was well, and the evil spirit departed from him" (ISam. 16:23).

But many of our gospel artists wave this away today by saying 'time has changed'. But whether time has changed or not, music is meant to minister to souls, refresh them and bring them closer to God.

Guest musicians invited to the church must be ready to display these characteristics:

* They must be people who really know the Lord and are living right.

* They must be under a pastor and be a strong member of a gospel church.

* They must stay to hear, listen and obey the word of God in their lives. Those who don't know, sing and live the word should not be encouraged in our pulpits.

* They must minister, not to tickle the ear but to touch the heart.

* They must be given honorarium at our discretion, not them charging for performance.

* Worldly and carnal Artists must never be allowed to minister in our pulpits.

* Sinful, wayward and immoral gospel artists who

only sing for money and show off should never be allowed in our Church.

* Commercialised artists who turn the grace and gifts of God into money venture should not be allowed on our altars.

GUEST PROPHETS

Every church will always need prophetic word from the Lord, however, the church must not be built on prophets and prophecies. Once in a while, true and godly prophets can be of great blessings to the church, but adequate care must be taken. Numerous examples abound where prophets and prophecies were used to cause disaffection in the church and disintegration was the outcome. While we should not despise prophets and prophecies, however, we must be careful that it doesn't result in church breakaway.

* Christian prophets that are living godly and unblameable lives can be allowed to minister in the church.

* Christian prophets that have a track record of hearing from the Lord can be welcomed in the church.

* Christian prophets must work closely and humbly with pastors and under pastors.

* Before prophetic words are released to the church, the pastor must be aware and approve it.

* Unbiblical and deceptive prophecies must never be allowed to thrive in the church.

* Those who have prophetic gifts should work closely with the senior pastor. They should stop having 'church within a church'.

* Every prophet and prophecy must be tested and tried in the light of God's word. Once it doesn't agree, it should be rejected.

The word of God is the greatest prophet we should all be subject to. The faith of people should not rest in prophets and prophecies but in the unchanging and undiluted word of God. Prophecies that lead to immorality, idol worship, sinful bondage and questionable practises should not be allowed or given room in the church.

> *Every church will always need prophetic word from the Lord, however, the church must not be built on prophets and prophecies*

For example, a prophet said the 'Lord' instructed him to cast out demons from the private part of women with his manhood!' That is absolute rubbish and demonic ways of sleeping with women. Another prophet said he received revelations that women that are looking for the fruit of the womb should come and pray with him nakedly. Of course, he slept with many of the desperate and gullible women and the church was the worse for it. Such deception and sinful tendencies must not be welcomed in our church, if we really want to please the Lord and be the true church of God.

"Notwithstanding, I have a few things against thee, because thou sufferest that woman Jezebel, which calleth herself a prophetess, to teach and to seduce my servants to commit fornication, and to eat things sacrificed unto idols. And I gave her space to repent of her fornication; and she repented not. Behold, I will cast her into a bed and them that commit adultery with her into great tribulation, except they repent of their deeds. And I will kill her children with death. And all the churches shall know that I am he which searcheth the reins and hearts: and I will give unto every one of you according to your works" (Rev. 2:20-23).

If we don't want the fiery judgement of the Lord to come upon the church, then we should try every prophet and prophecy in the light of the word of God. 'Thus says the Lord' is not enough for us to bow down and fear, we must test the wordings of the prophecy and life of the prophet, whether they are in line with the clear word of God in the Bible.

CHAPTER 1 3

LASTING IMPACT

BY GUEST MINISTERS

P hilip the Evangelist was drawn away from the revival in Samaria to preach to a lonely man on a desert road. He was invited by the Holy Spirit to minister to this African man of great authority. Philip honoured the invitation and did the job with his whole heart.

"Then the spirit said unto Philip, go near, and join thyself to this chariot. And Philip ran thither to him, and heard him read the prophet Esaias, and said, understandest thou what thou readest? And he said, How can I,

except some man should guide me? And he desired Philip that he would come up and sit with him... Then Philip opened his mouth, and began at the same scripture, and preached unto him Jesus. And as they went on their way, they came unto a certain water: and the eunuch said, see, here is water; what doth hinder me to be baptized? And Philip said, if thou believest with all thine heart, thou mayest. And he answered I believe that Jesus Christ is Son of God. And he commanded the chariot to stand still: and they went down both into the water: both Philip and the eunuch: and he baptised him" (Acts 8:29-31, 35-38).

The man got saved and history says he brought christianity to the Continent of Africa. The millions of souls that have known the Lord in Africa and from Africa today can be traced to Philip's response to the invitation to preach to the Eunuch on the desert road. If Philip had refused the prompting of the Holy Spirit to leave the revival in Samaria and go to one man on a lonely road, the gospel might not have gotten to Africa. The Lesson? No audience is too small to preach to. I think that can help some guest speakers that refused to preach to 'small' audience.

> **Value every opportunity to minister and determine to make impact with your ministrations**

Philip made a lasting impact through that one man. He did the work very well and today, the impact is still there for all to see. Making such monumental impact must be the goal and focus of every guest minister. Accept and honour invitations as the Lord leads you and see it as opportunity to affect lives for now and eternity. Value every opportunity to minister and determine to make impact with your ministrations. Celebreate the priviledge to share and take it as God-given opportunity to bless lives and affect generations to come. To make lasting impact with your ministrations, you should focus on the following:

1. Lead sinners to Christ

The greatest impact you can make is to bring somebody to Christ through your ministration. The worth of a saved soul is priceless, so go for it. Talk about sin, separation from God and the atoning work of Christ. Do like Philip the Evangelist. Lead people to Christ at every given opportunity. For years to come, that is an impact that cannot be easily erased.

2. Draw people back to God

Preach and focus on restoring backsliders back to God. Many people have backslided from the faith today due to sinful pleasures, crisis in their lives and deception of the devil. Let your ministration bring them back to God.

3. Revival of spiritual life

Your ministration in any church should focus on bringing the revival of God back to individual and corporate life of the church. Many are cold, lukewarm, carnal, ungodly and are only going through the routine of christian life today. Let your ministrations be used by God to revive such people. Many times, our physical and material blessings can become a curse that will draw us away from God. Many prosperous nations, cities, churches and families have experienced this curse already.

Your ministration in any church should focus on bringing the revival of God back to individual and corporate life of the church

Let your ministrations bring God's revival to such people and draw them back to God. More than ever before, revival must start from the church today.

4.   Prepare people for eternity

Making lasting impact also means that you should focus on getting people ready for the rapture. Whether we like it or not, the rapture will soon take place and we had better be ready for it. What better way to get people ready for eternity than reminding them of this truth and laying strong emphasis on it regularly. Then you can do a job for eternity.

5.   Raise them up for ministry and leadership

If you really want to make a lasting impact, use your opportunity to minister to equip the people for ministry and leadership. Strong teachings and providing resources for them will help in this aspect. Good guest ministers should have quality tapes, books, CD's and materials to give or sell at a very small amount to the potential leaders in the church. This will go a long way to help their spiritual and ministry developments. Preachings will be forgotten, but quality resources will speak for years to come.

6.   Equip the leader to do a better job

I've found out that the best way to impact a church, ministry and leader is to provide resources that will enable and empower them to do a better job. Conferences come and go. Meetings end and messages are forgotten, but quality materials, books, VCD's, tapes and write-ups will continue to speak as long as possible. God gave us the Bible for that purpose. He could have put all the Scriptures in our brains, but he decided to write and publish it, so that it can continue to minister to generations after generations. The lesson? Every dynamic and worthwhile guest minister must have books, materials and resources that will keep on blessing the people, long after the meetings have ended and forgotten. Over the years, that is what we have done in our Ministry and the testimonies have proved that this method works. I'm sorry for pastors, leaders, ministers and speakers who don't take time to produce quality resources. Their impact will be minimal and soon wipe off. Their story will be written in the sands of time, which can easily be erased. Your impact will only be unerasable when you have resources that will keep on blessing people. Help every leader you meet to do a better job by providing resources for them.

7.   Model a Christ-like life and good value

More than your preachings, ministrations and resources, your life makes a lasting impression - either positive or negative. Some people can preach powerfully, minister wonderfully and write beautifully, but they live sinful, ungodly, hypocritical and valueless lives.

> *Making lasting impact demands that you must live right. You cannot live wrong and lead right*

Making lasting impact demands that you must live right. You cannot live wrong and lead right. Your living will always affect your ministry and ministrations. Your private sins will soon catch up and ruin your public and ministerial life. Determine to live right. Live what you preach. Be a good example of the advise you give to others. Value integrity, honesty, humility and sincerity, so that you'll be credible and trustworthy. Long after you've ministered and gone, your life will still be speaking volumes in the heart and life of those who know you closely. So, model christlikeness in all you do.

Finally, let me leave you with these words; "what you know is not as important as what you do with what you know." Always practise operation BACK with them:

Believe these truths
Accept them into your life.
Copy them into your ministerial life.
Know them enough to practise them daily.

INTERNATIONAL CHURCH GROWTH MINISTRIES

INTERNATIONAL CHURCH GROWTH MINISTRIES was founded in 1994. The vision of the ministry is to provide current and reliable Church Growth principles in African context to Leaders, Pastors and Ministers that will lead to better and faster growth of their churches.

We do these through books, materials, VCD and audio cassettes at relatively low cost to people engaged in leading the church.

We equally organise seminars and conferences on various aspect of Church Growth and Health. We also accept invitations from churches to help analyse them, motivate their people and generally help the growth potentials of churches.

So far we have ministered to over 20,000 Pastors and Christian Workers across many denominational lines and independent churches. The results have been tremendous and the testimonies have been wonderful and interesting.

The ministry also saw the need to really raise the growth consciousness in the Continent and decided to pioneer an Institute on Church Growth. The response has been overwhelming as so many Pastors, General Overseers, and Church Leaders have enrolled to learn more about how to practically lead their churches to growth. The impact of the Institute on these Pastors' lives have started manifesting in the phenomenal growth of their churches and expansion of their ministries.

ICGM RESOURCES

If you found this book to be useful, you may be interested in some of the other resources available from ICGM.

Listed below are some of our books and resources:

Books:
1.   32 Strategic Ways to Increase Church attendance
2.   The Supernatural Leader
3.   Your Growth is Your Future
4.   The Secrets of Financially Strong Churches
5.   Our Churches and His Church
6.   Why Churches Breakaway & Lose members
7.   Strategic Living
8.   Leading Your Church to Lasting Growth
9.   22 Dynamic Laws of Church Growth
10.   Strategic Church Planting Today
11.   How to Support and Strengthen Your Pastors
12.   Leading From the Pulpit
13.   Spiritual Warfare for Dynamic Church Growth
14.   The Place of Anointing and Administration
15.   Family Growth
66.   Prayer Nugget
17.   Church Growth

18. Financial Growth
19. The Impact Driven Church
20. Grow the Pastor, Grow the Church
21. Personal Growth Today
22. The Loyal Associate

Resources:
a. Spiritual Warfare for church growth
b. Helping the clergy - leading your church to growth.
c. Practical church planting
d. Winning the society seminar
e. Mobilizing the laity
f. Warfare prayer for Growth
g. Closing the Backdoor of the church
h. Women ministry in church growth
i. Strategic level prayer for breakthrough
j. Signs and Wonders for church growth
k. Research and analysing of the church
l. How to grow a vibrant and Healthy churches
m. Why Churches Lose Members
n. Empowering the Church for 21st Century
o. Healthy Leadership for Healthy Churches
p. Tools for Tremendous and Transforming Ministry.
q. New Waves of God's Move for End Time Harvest
r. Magnetic, Multiplying, Marketable and Maximum Impact.
s. Building a Bigger, Better and Broader Church and many others.

Audio Tapes & VCD
1. Spiritual Warfare Series
2. Effective Ministers Series

3.   Women Ministry Series
4.   Closing the Backdoor Series
5.   Warfare Prayer Series
6.   Strategic Level Prayer Series
7.   Church Planting Series
8.   Healthy Church Series.

Journal:
Church Growth Journal is a quarterly teaching and news magazine that gives vital and practical information on how to grow the church.

For further information on these and other resources available, please write or contact us at our office or call the telephone lines provided in this book.

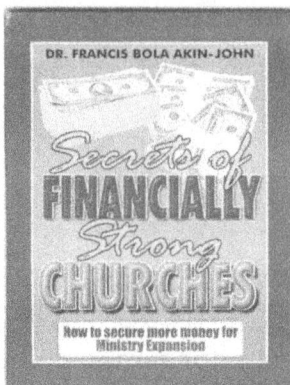

SECRETS OF FINANCIALLY STRONG CHURCHES
By: Francis Bola Akin-John

Do you still have problem raising money to effectively run your ministry or church? Or do you lack proper knowledge on how to manage it to achieve financial freedom for the church? Then this book is for you. It answers your questions about money, tells you why people give or don't give in your church and also offers practical solution to grow a debt - free and financially robust ministry. A must for you if you passionately desire financial buoyancy for your church.

22 DYNAMIC LAWS OF CHURCH GROWTH
By: Francis Bola Akin-John

Church growth is not a logical programme. It is a dynamic process made possible by strict adherence to various laws that guide durable, lasting and solid growth in the church. Violating any of these laws will cause retrogression and stagnation in the church, but an understanding of the laws enumerated in this well researched book will not only ensure growth in your church but it will also sustain the growth in any season. This book is a classic work and still one of the best materials from Africa's foremost Church Growth and Ministerial Consultant, by Francis Bola Akin-John.

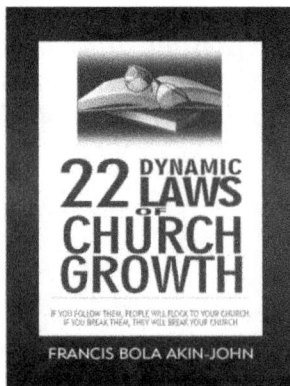

YOUR GROWTH IS YOUR FUTURE
By: Francis Bola Akin-John

Growth has no alternative. It is not optional. Your growth is your vehicle to the future. Your growth determines the level you will get to in life. If you desire success passionately either as a pastor, businessman or woman, student, corporate leader, trader, church worker, professional, house wife or church leader, this book is for you. Your personal growth precedes every other growth. Without growth you will become a person of yesterday, abort your greater future and open door for decay. This is a book for everybody.

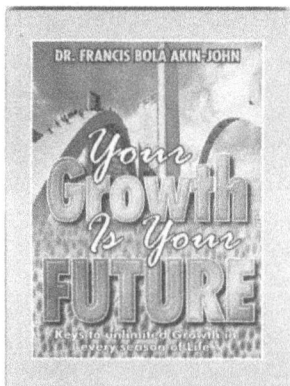

SUPERNATURAL POWER, MIRACLES, SIGNS & WONDERS TODAY
Dr. Francis Bola Akin-John

Many of the great growth of churches today are closely linked with the supernatural dimension of God. Without doubt, these are the days of God's power like never before. Every church and leader must key in to the supernatural move of God, if true and lasting church growth is to be seen and experienced.

This book by dr. Francis Bola Akin-John re-establishes the truth that every church leader can and should display the power of God's kingdom over that of the enemy.

Church leaders and ministers that really desire to operate in the supernatural realm of God must not only read, but also digest, study and soak up this book.

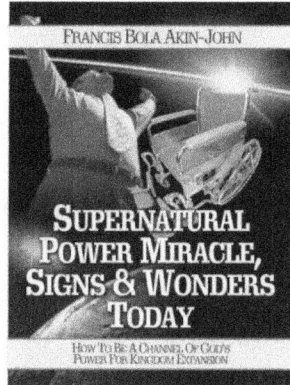

32 STRATEGIC WAYS TO INCREASE CHURCH ATTENDANCE
By: Francis Bola Akin-John

Church growth isn't automatic! It is achieved through the combination of spiritual, physical and environmental factors. By indepth research, coupled with rich personal experience as a pastor for many years, Dr. Akin-John highlights diverse strategies for numerical increase and growth in the church. If you read this book and prayerfully implement its content, you will discover that strategy is always better than energy. Get this book if you desire a passionate increase in your attendance. A must for every pastor!

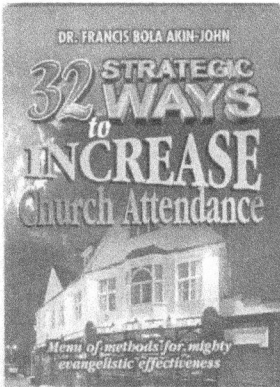

STRATEGIC CHURCH PLANTING TODAY
By: Francis Bola Akin-John

The last two decade witnessed an unprecedented church planting efforts by various Christian denominations, mission- minded individuals and independent ministers. In this book, Dr. Akin-John, himself a researcher on church and ministerial matters, chronicles these efforts and examines the need, method, cost implication, the passion, the benefits, mistakes, misconception, planning, timing, impact, location, the message and the messenger of church planting today. No one has approached church planting than the way this book has done. It is a vintage material from a vintage author.

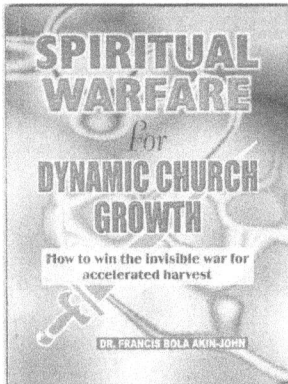

SPIRITUAL WARFARE FOR DYNAMIC CHURCH GROWTH
By: Francis Bola Akin-John

Achieving outstanding growth in your church is determined by how sharp your attacking instruments of warfare are. The war for control over the territory where your church is located must start in the spirit and end in the spirit. To have peace in your life, family and ministry, you must prepare for war. You must enforce growth and increase by violence in the spirit through all levels of spiritual warfare. Dr. Bola Akin-John made the subject matter more practical than theory here, with strong warning that harvest will tarry in your church unless you are willing to go all out against the visible and invisible powers of the enemy.

GROW THE PASTOR GROW THE CHURCH
By: Francis Bola Akin-John

The pastor is the number one key to the growth of the church. The pastor must be trained for maximum impact making in the church. An ungroomed pastor is much more dangerous to the church than the church is to him. This is because the church will be strong if the pastor is strong, the church will be prayerful if the pastor is prayerful, the church will be holy if the pastor is holy, the church will be weak if the pastor is weak and the church will grow if the pastor is growing. This book must not be missing in your library if you are a pastor that has other pastors or leaders within your leadership scope.

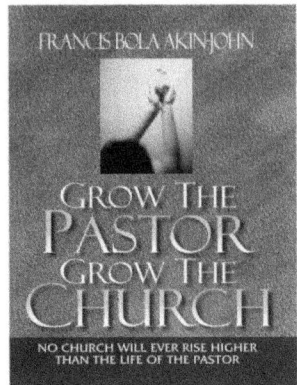

LEADING YOUR CHURCH TO LASTING GROWTH
By: Francis Bola Akin-John

Much more than the influx of people into your church and the excitement of ministering to a large crowd, this book unfolds to you powerful strategies necessary to sustain the growth.
Dr. Akin-John goes further to share with you time and field tested biblical principles that will ensure lasting growth and increase in your church.

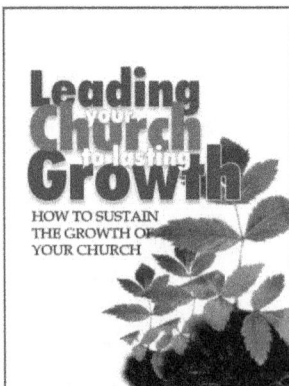

HOW TO SUPPORT AND STRENGTHEN YOUR PASTOR
By: Francis Bola Akin-John

No church can grow and experience all round increase without the faithful and collective contributions of her members. Unfortunately, many Christians know next to nothing about how to uphold and support their pastors. Here, the author spells out the responsibilities of every church member, associate leaders and heads of various church departments to their pastor - knowing fully well that what makes a good pastor is often the support of good people around him.

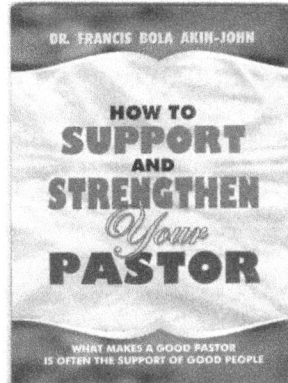

THE IMPACT DRIVEN CHURCH
By: Francis Bola Akin-John

The church is the only designated God's property on the surface of the earth. It was birthed to meet human needs and stand in the gap between man and God. Any church that does not align with this position can not make impact in this end time. Your church must make impact in the environment where it is located in order to be relevant in the community. It must stop existing as a mere figure but a force. In this book, Dr. Francis Bola Akin-John discusses with you how to make impact and be driven by same.

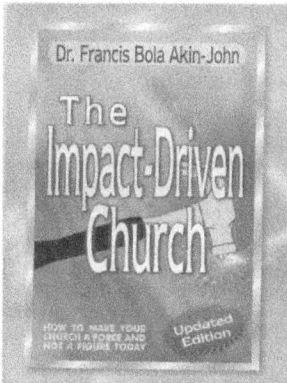

WHY CHURCHES BREAKAWAY AND LOSE MEMBERS
By: Francis Bola Akin-John

The rate at which churches breakaway is almost the same rate churches are being planted. The problem has grown to endemic proportions in the last couple of years, affecting every church either old or new. As a foremost Consultant on ministry and church matters, the author examines the causes of breakaway and membership loses in churches and proffers lasting solutions that will arrest chaos, retrogression, split and membership loses. This is a book every church Founder, General Overseer, Apostle, Superintendent, State and Regional Pastor, Senior Pastor and whoever intends to start a fresh work should read.

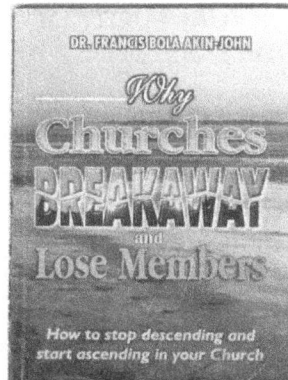

THE PLACE OF ANOINTING AND ADMINISTRATION IN CHURCH GROWTH
By: Francis Bola Akin-John

The sustainable growth of the church of Christ have been gravely affected by wrong notions on the dual issue of Anointing and Administration. It has been discovered that there is lack of balance in the church as regards each of these two areas.

The principles highlighted in this wonderful book provide the needed balanced approach on the issue of Anointing and Administration.

Read it for your edification and practise it for your promotion.

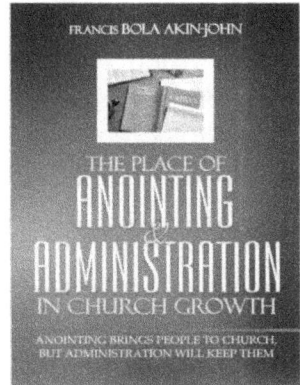

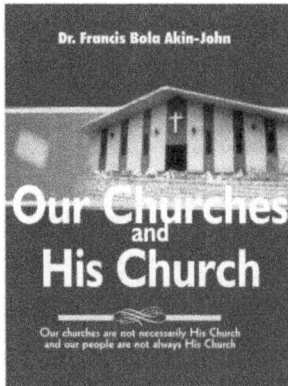

OUR CHURCHES AND HIS CHURCH
By: Francis Bola Akin-John

This book is an attempt to put a hand on the crisis that has engulfed the church today. Many practices, methods and models have clearly shown that our 'churches' are not necessarily His church. Many of what we call 'church' today are too far from what Christ had in mind when He said; "I will build my church ". Likewise, many of the people in 'churches' today cannot be said to be His people simply because majority of them do not really know Him.

Therefore, if you are really concerned about building His church, and you want to do a work that will not get burnt up, this book is for you! Every Senior Pastor, Bishop, General Overseer and Pastor must read this book over and over again and change where necessary.

SEXUAL PURITY IN LEADERSHIP
Dr. Francis Bola Akin-John

Either you like it or not, you will come across sexual pressure in your life and leadership. Leaders that are too simple, innocent and ignorant of the ravages of sexual pressure will surely fall into this trap of the enemy. Many great evangelists, preachers, pastors, bishops and church leaders have lost their anointing and ministry on the laps of strange women.

Sexual Purity in Leadership by Dr. Francis Bola Akin-John exposes the destructive and deadly sexual traps employ by satan against leaders and ministers of God and provides ways to avoid them. It is a must read for every success-minded leader.

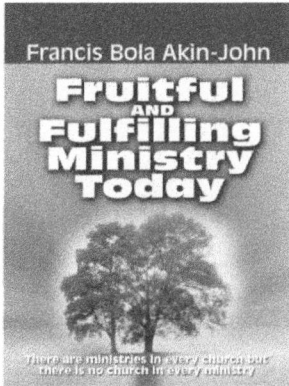

FRUITFUL AND FULFILLING MINISTRY TODAY
By: Francis Bola akin-John

This book is a tool that will help your ministry to move to the next level. Your ministry is the vehicle you are driving, you need tools to keep it running effectively and fast.

The quickness and durability of your ministry is determined by the tools of ministry at your disposal. Tools will help you to be effective, result oriented, impactful, creative, fruitful and to have tremendous and transforming ministry.

Those tools are scattered throughout in this book. Grab the ones you need by reading, studying, digesting and practising the insights in the book, so that you will no longer work as fools. It is only fools that lack real, genuine, relevant and creative tools for life and ministry.

THE LOYAL ASSOCIATE
By: Francis Bola Akin-John

This book is Dr. Francis bola Akin-John humble effort at establishing a right type of relationship between the leader and his associates, providing the right atmosphere for it and bringing sanity into the ungodly madness of unfaithful, disloyal and undependable associates.

It is appropriate for topmost leaders, useful and insightful for those in the middle leadership and challenging to those at the lowest rung of the ladder. If you can adapt and adjust to the timely truth of this book, you will save yourself from many hurts and heartaches.

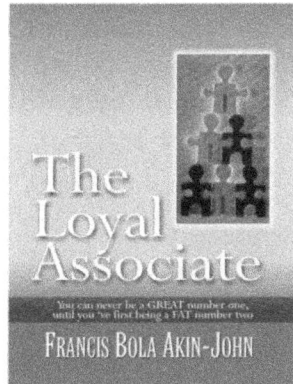

PERSONAL GROWTH TODAY
By: Francis Bola akin-John

Dr. Francis Bola Akin-John in this book revealed that the gap between a person's vision and present reality can only be filled through commitment to his personal development. And that personal growth prevents personal and professional stagnation, and surely impacts organisational growth. If you want to reach the height of your potential, personally and professionally, then commit yourself to daily personal improvement.

Personal Growth Today is a classic that must not be missed. Read, study and digest this book over and over again. Drink deep from it and let it become part and parcel of your daily living.

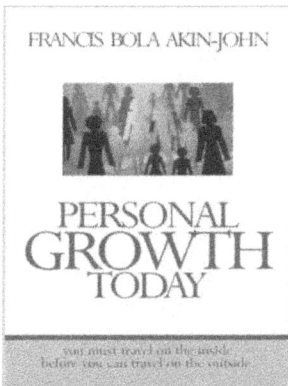

FEEDBACK

Questions, comments and contact about this book should be directed to:

International Chruch Growth Ministry
332, Abeokuta Expressway, Super B/stop,
Oke-Odo, Agege P.O. Box 3747, Oshodi, Lagos State.
234-1-8976100, 08023000714, 08029744296
e-mail:- akingrow@yahoo.com
website: churchgrowthafrica.org.